Understanding Open
Source Software Development

To Bob and Tanja
               – JF

To the memory of Diarmuid
               – BF

Understanding Open Source Software Development

Joseph Feller

Brian Fitzgerald

ADDISON-WESLEY

An imprint of PEARSON EDUCATION

London • Boston • Indianapolis • New York • Mexico City • Toronto •
Sydney • Tokyo • Singapore • Hong Kong • Cape Town • New Delhi •
Madrid • Paris • Amsterdam • Munich • Milan • Stockholm

PEARSON EDUCATION LIMITED

Head Office:
Edinburgh Gate
Harlow CM20 2JE
England
Tel: +44 (0)1279 623623
Fax: +44 (0)1279 431059

London Office:
128 Long Acre
London WC2E 9AN
England
Tel: +44 (0)20 7447 2000
Fax: +44 (0)20 7240 5771

Websites: www.it-minds.com
www/aw.com/cseng

First published in Great Britain in 2002

© Pearson Education Limited 2002

The rights of Joseph Feller and Brian Fitzgerald to be identified as the authors
of this Work have been asserted by them in accordance with the Copyright,
Designs and Patents Act 1988.

ISBN: 0–201–73496–6

British Library Cataloguing in Publication Data
A CIP catalogue record for this book can be obtained from the British Library.

Library of Congress Cataloging in Publication Data
Applied for.

Many of the designations used by manufacturers and sellers to distinguish their
products are claimed as trademarks. Pearson Education Limited has made every
attempt to supply trademark information about manufacturers and their
products mentioned in this book. Trademark notice appears on p. ix.

10 9 8 7 6 5 4 3 2 1

Typeset by Land & Unwin (Data Sciences) Ltd, Bugbrooke, Northants
Printed and bound in Great Britain by Biddles Ltd of Guildford and King's
Lynn

The publisher's policy is to use paper manufactured from sustainable forests.

Contents

Trademark notice

Microsoft Windows®, Internet Explorer™, Office 2000®, Outlook Express®, and Visual Basic™ are trademarks and registered trademarks of Microsoft Corporation.

Java™ is a trademark of Sun Microsystems, Incorporated.

JavaScript™ is a trademark of Sun Microsystems, Incorporated used under license for technology invented and implemented by Netscape.

COBOL™ and COBOL Workbench™ are trademarks of Micro Focus.

Unix® is a registered trademark licensed through X/OPEN Co. Ltd. (Collaboration of Novell, HP and SCO)

Dreamweaver™ and Cold Fusion™ are trademarks of Macromedia Incorporated.

Apple®, Mac OS X®, Quicktime®, and Dylan™ are registered trademarks and trademarks of Apple Computer, Incorporated.

386-386/ix™ is a trademark of Interactive Systems, Incorporated.

AS400™, OS/2®, APL™, DB2™, and Websphere™ are registered trademarks and trademarks of International Business Machines (IBM) Corporation.

Netscape Communicator™ and Netscape Navigator™ are trademarks of Netscape Communication Corporation.

Eiffel™ is a trademark of Nonprofit International Consortium for Eiffel.

Objective C™ is a trademark of StepStone Corporation.

SMALLTALK® is a registered trademark of Xerox Corporation.

Fortran® and Pascal® are registered trademarks of Oracle Corp UK Ltd.

Erlang™ is a trademark of Ericsson Utvecklings AB.

LOGOS™ is a trademark of LOGOS Corporation.

Progress™ is a trademark of Progress Software Corporation.

Prolog™ is a trademark of Expert Systems International.

Simula™ is a trademark of Simula AS.

Lotus® is a registered trademark of Lotus Development Corporation.

Delphi™ is a trademark of Borland International Corporation.

Acknowledgments

Extracts pp. 97, 97–8 and 99 from Magnus Bergquist and Jan Ljungberg (2001) "The power of gifts: organising social relationships in open source communities," *Information Systems Journal*, **11**, 4; reproduced with permission from Blackwell Publishing, Oxford.

Extract pp. 164–6 from N. Bezroukov (1999) "Open source software as a special type of academic research (a critique of vulgar Raymondism)," *First Monday*, **4**, 10.

Foreword

This book marks the end of the beginning in our understanding of Open Source development. Until it appeared, all the attempts at a really comprehensive description of the phenomenon had come from Open Source hackers like myself, theorists operating from within the culture we were describing.

We had the advantage of knowing our ground, but the disadvantage of knowing it perhaps too well – there are undoubtedly good questions we would never have thought to ask. That's why I've hoped from the beginning that an analytical literature about open source, independent of the Open Source community itself, would evolve.

While other outside analysts and academics have tackled specific subtopics, Joe Feller and Brian Fitzgerald have given us the first book-length attempt that I am aware of to marshal approaches from multiple disciplines (software engineering theory, sociology, business analysis) into a portrait of the whole.

This book is not the last word; last words are about dead things, and Open Source development is quite lustily alive, But it is an important step along the way, answering some questions and raising others that will continue to be live and fruitful research topics.

Welcome to the conversation ...

Eric S. Raymond

http://www.tuxedo.org/~esr/

Introduction

Since the coining of the term Open Source Software (OSS) in February 1998 (Open Source Initiative, 2001b), we have witnessed a surge of academic and scientific interest in the topic. The earliest analytical accounts of the phenomenon actually predate the use of the Open Source label, at which time Richard Stallman's term "Free Software" was more commonly used to describe software like the Linux operating system and the BIND DNS Server. While extremely insightful and highly influential, these early accounts tended to be

- journalistic, e.g., the investigative reporting of Glyn Moody (1997);

- ambassadorial, e.g., the early writings of Eric Raymond (1997); or

- ideological, e.g., the work of Richard Stallman (1985).

Likewise, the essays in what are perhaps the most widely cited books on OSS, *Open Sources* (DiBona *et al.*, 1999) and *The Cathedral and the Bazaar* (Raymond, 2001[1]), are generally subjective accounts of the phenomenon written by key participants in the Free Software and OSS movements.

Beginning in 1998, we begin to see the proliferation of more rigorous academic and scientific treatments of OSS, coming from

---

[1] Eric Raymond has written much on Open Source Software, and his classic essays have evolved over time. Most are collected in the 2001 book, *The Cathedral and the Bazaar*. However, these were originally published several years before – *The Cathedral and the Bazaar* was originally published in April 1997, for example. To allow greater transparency in referencing, we have annotated the Raymond references throughout the book by appending an acronym as follows: BHH – Brief History of Hackerdom; CatB – Cathedral and the Bazaar; HtS – Homesteading the Noosphere; JF – Jargon File; MC – Magic Cauldron; RotH – Revenge of the Hackers.

researchers and practitioners in a number of disciplines, but primarily from those involved in the study of software engineering and information systems development. This research has appeared in a number of major peer-reviewed journals and conferences, including *Communications of the ACM, First Monday, Information Systems Journal, IEE Proceedings – Software; IEEE Internet Computing, IEEE Software, European Journal of Information Systems, American Conference on Information Systems, European Conference on Information Systems, International Conference on Information Systems*, and *International Conference on Software Engineering*, to name just a few.

Our goal in writing this book was to provide a useful, accurate, and provocative one-stop reference for researchers, students, developers, and managers who need to grasp the big picture of both OSS and OSS scholarship – from the seminal accounts to the most up-to-date research on the topic.

Why we wrote this book

If we consider the question "Why study Open Source Software?" there are a number of answers. Firstly, a somewhat superficial, but nonetheless valid answer – we should study it because it seems that everyone (companies, investors, governments, etc.) is excited about it. From this perspective, the recent surge of academic inquiry into OSS is not at all surprising – the global research community has, in fact, been jumping onto a bandwagon that was already quite crowded.

One easily quantifiable measure of the general enthusiasm for OSS is the adoption of Open Source *products* by companies, organizations, and individuals. As of April 2001, the award-winning (Apache Software Foundation, 2001d) Apache HTTP Server ran over 62 percent of 28.5 million websites queried by Netcraft (2001a). Likewise, as of December 2000 the Linux operating system accounted for 27 percent of the enterprise server market and, although Linux has less market share than Microsoft Windows (which held 41 percent at that time), its market share is growing at a faster rate (Shankland, 2001). It is equally significant to note the adoption of

Open Source *processes* by large traditional software houses like Apple, IBM, Netscape, SGI, and Sun Microsystems (IBM alone has announced plans to spend $1 billion supporting OSS development in 2001[2]). In short, OSS products and processes are enjoying quite a warm reception in the general software market, and are predicted to make quite a long-term impact; Forrester Research, for example, has estimated that the cost of software will drop 20 percent by 2004 due to OSS.[3]

Open Source has also had some dramatic successes in the stock market. In 1999, Red Hat's[4] Initial Public Offering (IPO) was nothing short of remarkable, with common stock rising in value by 300 percent on the first day of trading. Even though at the time Red Hat only had revenues of less than $10m and had not yet shown a profit,[5] at the end of the first day's trading Red Hat had a capital value of nearly $3 billion (Shankland, 1999). However, even this performance pales when compared with the IPO, just a few weeks later, of VA Linux[6] which experienced a 700 percent increase – *the largest single day gain in US stock market history* (Kawamoto and Shankland, 1999). In 2001, OSS companies like Red Hat and VA Linux are, of course, suffering along with the rest of the high-tech world. Stock prices have fallen, lay-offs have occurred, and a few OSS companies, like Eazel,[7] have recently closed their doors for good. Just the same, the message is very clear – investors in 1999–2000 saw Open Source as the 'dotcom-like' gold mine of the future.

OSS has even received support from major world governments. The People's Republic of China, for example, sees OSS as a way to break away from Microsoft's (and the West's) control over software

---

[2] *New York Times*, March 20, 2000.

[3] *The Economist*, April 12, 2001.

[4] Red Hat is one of the most successful distributors and support providers for the Linux operating system.

[5] As of Q1 of fiscal year 2002, Red Hat has revenues of $25.6m and is showing a profit of approximately $600,000 (Red Hat, 2001a).

[6] At the time of their IPO, VA Linux was primarily a hardware systems vendor. However, in June 2001, the company shifted their focus to software and services (VA Linux, 2001).

[7] http://www.eazel.com.

(Smith, 2000). Meanwhile, a panel of the President's Information Technology Advisory Committee advised the US federal government to back OSS "as an alternate path for software development for high end computing" (PITAC, 2000). Open Source has even popped up in US election politics. Former Vice-President Al Gore used the first "Open Source" presidential campaign website (**www.algore2000.com,** now defunct); the site's back-end source code was opened to the community of developers who might be inclined to support the Democratic Party in this unique fashion.

As noted above, the popularity of OSS is interesting, exciting, even entertaining, but it is not the best reason to research the topic. A more durable answer to the question "Why study Open Source Software?" requires us to go *behind* the successes of OSS discussed above. Linux and Apache are not major players in their respective market sectors just because they can be acquired at little or no cost. In fact, since the major proportion of the total cost of software development is incurred in the maintenance phase – with reliable estimates ranging from 70 percent (Boehm, 1976) to 80 percent (Flaatten *et al.*, 1989) – the sticker price of software is somewhat irrelevant. These products (and others like BIND, Sendmail, and Perl) are successful because software users recognize the quality and stability of the products, the economic advantages of shared cost and shared risk in software ownership, and the technological advantages of building open and modifiable platforms.

It is the strengths (and also shortcomings) of OSS as a process for developing software that makes rigorous research critical. OSS makes use of software development methods that are at first glance at odds with many traditional engineering paradigms. Likewise, OSS has a set of business and economic assumptions that often appear antithetical to traditional software industry models. Just the same, the OSS process has produced several examples of highly competitive software, has enabled the launch of numerous pure-play companies,[8] and has changed the strategic tack of some of the

---

[8] A pure-play OSS company is one that exclusively deals in OSS products or services.

world's largest proprietary software corporations. Since it is not possible simply to dismiss OSS as insignificant, or faddish, it has become necessary to find accurate answers to questions like "what is the OSS development method?", "under what circumstances does it work?", "how sustainable is it?", "what tools enable it?", etc.

Who should read this book?

When we undertook this project, we wanted to produce a book that would be useful to both academic and professional readers.

On the academic side, we have endeavored to provide the professional research community with a thorough synthesis and analysis of the OSS research that has appeared to date. If you are a member of this community, we hope that you'll find *Understanding Open Source Software Development* to be a powerful springboard as you pursue your own investigations of OSS. We feel that graduate and advanced undergraduate students engaging in research will be able to use the book in a similar fashion. We also wanted to create a volume that would be suitable as a teaching text. As we were writing, we tried to keep in mind the needs of students and faculty involved in software engineering, systems development, software business, and socio-technological course work.

On the professional side, we wanted to disseminate the significant volume of rigorous academic research into OSS development practices back into the development community. The software development community suffers as much as any other contemporary group from information overload. While there has certainly been an increase in research on the software engineering issues of OSS, there has not necessarily been a comparable heightening of awareness *about* this research in the wider development community. The desire for the dissemination of research back into the OSS community is evident in the conversations of that community. For example, in the quite recent past, James Tauber (1999), a senior developer with the highly respected Apache Software Foundation, wrote:

> There have been numerous musings on the business and anthropology of Open Source. Is anyone aware of readings that address the actual software engineering issues?

Finally, we wanted to provide managers and business strategists with a more solid understanding of the technologies and methods associated with OSS. As noted above, the investment and entrepreneurial communities have perceived Open Source as a road to rapid and phenomenal success, but how much is actually understood about the delicate relationship between software as a business and the OSS development process? Of particular importance is an understanding of OSS communities. As Michael Tiemann (Dougherty and Sims, 2000), CTO of Red Hat, Inc. and co-founder of Cygnus Corporation, puts it,

> Money is just the gas, and the engine is the Open Source development community. And the quality of the people who are in that community determines how much horse-power this movement's going to have.

We believe it is critical that managers understand the complex system that is OSS development – as well as the unique strengths and weaknesses of the technologies produced by that process – if they are to successfully embrace Open Source.

How this book is organized

The first three chapters of this book can be thought of as an Open Source primer, and are intended mainly to bring readers approaching the subject for the first time up to speed. Hopefully, OSS veterans will also find it a useful summary of the topic. Chapter 1, *Overview of Open Source Software*, summarizes the Open Source Definition – the set of distribution terms with which a license must comply for the software to be considered Open Source – and provides an overview of representative OSS licenses, products, development methods, and processes. Chapter 2, *A history of Open Source Software*, discusses the historical events and trends that led to the contemporary Open Source movement. Finally, Chapter 3, *The landscape of Open Source Software*, offers a roadmap of the major companies and organizations involved in OSS today.

We then come to the core of the book, namely the analysis of Open Source Software. We begin in Chapter 4, *Deriving a framework for analyzing Open Source Software*, by examining two influential frameworks, Zachman's framework for IS architecture, and Checkland's CATWOE framework from the Soft Systems Method. Based on these theoretical models, we derive a framework for analyzing five major aspects of OSS. In Chapters 5 through 9 we then apply the analytical framework, asking questions like:

- What defines a software system as OSS?

- How is the OSS process organized and managed?

- Who are the developers and organizations involved?

- Where and when does OSS development take place?

- What are the motivations behind OSS development?

Finally, in Chapter 10, *Critical questions and future research*, we consider some of the questions raised by the information in the previous chapters. We discuss the strengths and weaknesses of OSS development, the apparent paradoxes that characterize it, and offer our recommendations for future research.

Visit us online

Understanding Open Source Software Development is complemented by the *Open Source Resources* website at **http://opensource.ucc.ie/**. We would like to see *Open Source Resources* become a valuable OSS research portal. On the site, you'll find regularly maintained links to OSS companies, organizations, projects, news, opinion, research, and events.

Please feel free to contact us directly by email at **jfeller@afis.ucc.ie** and **bf@ucc.ie**.

We hope you enjoy *Understanding Open Source Software Development*!

Acknowledgments

We would like to thank our reviewers – Danese Cooper (Sun Microsystems), Frank Hecker (Collab.Net), Scott Hissam (Software Engineering Institute, Carnegie Mellon University), Tony Lawrie (Centre for Software Reliability, University of Newcastle upon Tyne), and Jan Ljungberg (Viktoria Institute, University of Gothenburg) – for their thorough reviews, thoughtful suggestions, and wealth of knowledge of the OSS domain. Their comments and corrections were invaluable in the preparation of this book. While we might like to blame any mistakes and inaccuracies on them and others, such errors are, of course, our responsibility alone.

Joseph Feller
Brian Fitzgerald
October 2001

Overview of Open Source Software

In this chapter, we provide a high-level introduction to Open Source Software. Specifically, we discuss the nine criteria of the Open Source Definition (OSD), examine some OSD-compliant licenses, identify some examples of Open Source Software products, and briefly characterize the OSS development process. We begin with a very brief synopsis of "everything you wanted to know about software source code but were afraid to ask," just in case this critical concept is unfamiliar.

What is software source code?

Computer software is initially created as a set of instructions, written in a programming language like C or Java. These instructions are referred to as the source, or source code, of the software. In order for the software to actually run on a computer, it must first be compiled, that is, converted into binary form (a string of 1s and 0s). This is because at the fundamental level a computer can only deal with electrical switches, which may be on or off, 1 or 0 representing these states respectively. The restriction to just two states, 1 and 0, gives rise to the term binary code. While being restricted to such a limited binary vocabulary might seem to be a huge constraint, computers achieve the astonishing things they do by being able to manipulate these binary configurations many millions of times per second. Thus, these binary configurations can be constructed into very large, sophisticated programs.

The earliest programmers (including one of the authors) wrote software directly at the binary level (called a first-generation programming language (1GL)) by necessity. This was, of course, an extremely frustrating process, where a single transposed 1 or 0, completely undetectable to the naked eye, represents a bug that prevents the program from running. This mode of programming was barely tolerable if you were a research scientist, which many of the earliest programmers were (see Chapter 2), but when the computer began to spread to a business context in the 1950s and '60s, it became a considerable problem. The first solution was the creation of second-generation languages (2GLs), i.e., a language comprising short three-letter mnemonics which could represent commands that the computer would operate on, e.g., MOV (move), STA (store accumulator), LDA (load accumulator), etc. These second-generation languages were called assembly languages, the assembler being an actual computer program that could transform the "user-friendly" mnemonics into the correct sequence of 1s and 0s required to ultimately run the software. Assembly language programs were readable by humans – just about. A 30,000-byte (a byte being itself a precise configuration of eight 1s and 0s) program might be represented in 200 lines of assembly language. However, the price of such "user-friendliness" was that the language produced software that ran slightly less efficiently. Thus, some milliseconds of performance degradation, or some less efficient use of memory or storage might occur – all very serious problems when you were trying to operate with something like 4K of primary memory.

Assembly language was not all that readable (although "old" programmers will often express wistful longing for a return to this "real programming" but largely probably because it was such an esoteric power-base), and so, towards the end of the 1950s, third-generation languages (3GLs) started to appear, COBOL (Common Business Oriented Language) and the like. These were considerably easier to program in – a 30,000-byte binary program in 1s and 0s which could require 200 lines of assembly might only require 20 lines of a third-generation language. However, 3GL programs again sacrificed much in terms of efficiency when they were translated into the binary code of 1s and 0s. This transformation of a 3GL to binary was done automatically by a computer program called a compiler (which does not make any mistakes in the translation, despite the difficulty).

As programming spread to the wider user community in the 1970s and '80s, the so-called fourth-generation languages (4GLs) emerged. While more readable and user-oriented, these sacrificed still more in terms of run-time efficiency. Thus, in programs where performance was critical, programmers still tended to use assembly languages, as this allowed them to engage more closely and efficiently with the computer's internal functioning.

The real breakthrough in computer programming emerged with the third-generation language, C, developed at AT&T by a small team which included Dennis Ritchie who also co-developed the Unix operating system (see Chapter 2). Being a 3GL, the C language was much easier to program in than assembly language, but did not sacrifice any of the low-level access to the computer's internal functioning that is required to eke the best performance from the computer. Thus, pretty much all the infrastructure software (operating systems, utilities, and the like) that runs on computers nowadays has been programmed in C.

Getting back to the point, there were two completely serendipitous outcomes of the use of binary mode for software distribution, both of which made it attractive to commercial software development organizations. Firstly, programs that contain millions of lines of source code (3GL or 4GL), when compiled into binary code, occupy much less storage space (they are stored more efficiently). Secondly, and more importantly, binary code offers privacy; it is well nigh impossible to decipher even a small program in binary code. It is, of course, also effectively impossible to make any modifications to software in its binary form. Hence, software is generally distributed in binary form by proprietary software companies in order to preserve their privacy. At the heart of the Open Source and Free Software movements is the principle that the software source code, not just binary distributions, should be available so that both understanding and modifying the software is possible.

The Open Source Definition

Nobody owns or controls the term "Open Source," as it was deemed too broad and descriptive to be a trademark under US law.[1] However, in general use (and in this book), *Open Source Software is software distributed under terms that comply with the Open Source Definition.* The OSD is a document maintained by the Open Source Initiative (OSI). In Chapter 5, we will further justify the use of the OSD and discuss some of the problems of defining OSS at some length. Here, we simply offer a quick overview of the OSD.

It is important to note that the Open Source Definition is not a license in itself. Rather, it is a specification against which a software product's "terms of distribution" can be measured. Terms of distribution include both the software's license and the way in which the software is distributed (e.g., is the source code actually being made available?). If a software product's terms of distribution are found to comply with the OSD, that product may be said to be Open Source. Furthermore, it is eligible to bear the *OSI Certified* certification mark (Perens, 1999; Open Source Initiative, 2001d). It should also be noted that the OSD is an all-or-nothing specification. Software distributed under terms that conform to only part of the OSD (even if it conforms to eight out of the nine criteria) is not Open Source and cannot be *OSI Certified* (Perens, 1999; Open Source Initiative, 2001c).

According to the OSI, the *OSI Certified* certification mark "applies to software, not to licenses" (Open Source Initiative, 2001d).

---

[1] It has been argued that the term Open Source was not *originally* too broad and descriptive, but became so through the initial mismanagement of the term. See Rosen (2001).

However, in practice, the OSD has been used mainly as a licensing standard, and the OSI maintain a list of OSD-compliant licenses (Open Source Initiative, 2001a). The majority of OSS products in circulation are *self-certified* (they are distributed under the terms of a previously approved license, and are thus implicitly trusted to implement it properly) and are not evaluated by the OSI on a product-by-product basis. Developers may also, of course, submit a new license for OSI approval. Either way, the *OSI Certified* mark is used by attaching one of two notices to the software product, namely, "This software is OSI Certified Open Source Software. OSI Certified is a certification mark of the Open Source Initiative." or, simply, "OSI Certified Open Source Software." (Open Source Initiative, 2001d).

The Open Source Definition (Open Source Initiative, 2001c) begins:

Introduction
Open Source doesn't just mean access to the source code. The distribution terms of open-source software must comply with the following criteria:

1. Free Redistribution
The license shall not restrict any party from selling or giving away the software as a component of an aggregate software distribution containing programs from several different sources. The license shall not require a royalty or other fee for such sale.

The first OSD criterion, Free Redistribution, asserts the user's right to redistribute the software in any way he or she sees fit, which includes the selling of the software. Since the OSI is deeply committed to both the widespread commercial adoption of OSS and the Free Software roots from which it emerged (see Chapter 2), this clause is quite important.

2. Source Code
The program must include source code, and must allow distribution in source code as well as compiled form. Where some form of a product is

not distributed with source code, there must be a well-publicized means of obtaining the source code for no more than a reasonable reproduction cost – preferably, downloading via the Internet without charge. The source code must be the preferred form in which a programmer would modify the program. Deliberately obfuscated source code is not allowed. Intermediate forms such as the output of a preprocessor or translator are not allowed.

The second criterion explicitly requires the availability of source code. One of the key technological strengths of OSS is the ability for users to evaluate and modify the underlying source code. For this to occur, the code must be made available along with the compiled software. The sub-clause disallowing "deliberately obfuscated source code" and "intermediate forms" emphasizes again the fact that it is not just the license, but the full terms of a software product's distribution, being evaluated *vis-à-vis* the *OSI Certified* mark. Freedom of redistribution and availability of source code are perhaps the two most well-known characteristics of Open Source Software.

3. Derived Works
The license must allow modifications and derived works, and must allow them to be distributed under the same terms as the license of the original software.

This third criterion, Derived Works, extends the usefulness of visible source code by requiring that it be freely modifiable, and that modifications can be redistributed. The OSI is a pragmatic, rather than ideological group, and the third criterion highlights this mindset. The ability to view source code may be educational, but it is far from revolutionary. Rather, it is the user's ability to modify the source code that supports the somewhat key OSS development processes, like peer review and parallel development. Perens (1999) puts it another way, noting that software "has little use if you can't maintain it" and that the ability to modify software is a prerequisite for maintaining it.

It is important to note that different OSD-compliant licenses deal differently with the terms of distribution for derived works. The GNU[2] General Public License (GPL), for example, is viral,[3] in that it requires derived works also to carry the GPL. Other licenses, like the Berkeley Software Distribution (BSD) License, allow developers to distribute modifications and derived works under different, even non-OSD compliant, terms.

4. Integrity of The Author's Source Code

The license may restrict source-code from being distributed in modified form only if the license allows the distribution of "patch files" with the source code for the purpose of modifying the program at build time. The license must explicitly permit distribution of software built from modified source code. The license may require derived works to carry a different name or version number from the original software.

Balancing the open-ended ability to modify software mandated in the third criterion, this fourth clause requires that the work of individual developers and maintainers be represented in an accurate manner. Many OSS products achieve this by requiring that the original application be redistributed in an unmodified form and accompanied by software patches that modify the application at build time. Another compromise is found in terms of distributions that allow modification of the base code, but require that derived products carry a different name from the original software. The freedom to use, change, sell, or give away the software, the availability of source code, and the protection of authors' intellectual property rights are the central tenets of the OSD.

The remaining criteria of the definition are used to head off loopholes and potential abuses. They are as follows:

---

[2] GNU stands for GNU's Not Unix – an example of a recursive acronym (where the first letter stands for the acronym itself), a popular practice in the software hacker community.

[3] A term which carries unfortunately negative connotations.

5. No Discrimination Against Persons or Groups

The license must not discriminate against any person or group of persons.

6. No Discrimination Against Fields of Endeavor

The license must not restrict anyone from making use of the program in a specific field of endeavor. For example, it may not restrict the program from being used in a business, or from being used for genetic research.

Criteria five and six explicitly address the issue of discrimination. Again, the OSI goal is to open up the OSS process to the maximum number of users and developers. This means that OSD-compliant licenses may not impose ideological or other restrictions on software use. Although the OSI sees these criteria as protecting the freedom of individuals and companies to use OSS products in commercial endeavors, Perens (1999) frames it in wider terms, stating that

> Your software must be equally usable in an abortion clinic, or by an anti-abortion organization. These political arguments belong on the floor of Congress, not in software licenses. Some people find this lack of discrimination extremely offensive.

The seventh criterion proactively asserts the enduring validity of the license down the chain of users, as follows:

7. Distribution of License

The rights attached to the program must apply to all to whom the program is redistributed without the need for execution of an additional license by those parties.

The OSI rationale behind this clause was to make it impossible for anyone along this chain to "close" an OSS product. Perens (1999) points out that no-signature-required licenses borrow from both contract law and copyright law, while Rosenberg (2000) notes that this line of thinking has precedent in real estate law, where parties are bound by contracts which they may not have been involved in making.

Finally, the last two criteria are closely related. They are,

8. License Must Not Be Specific to a Product

The rights attached to the program must not depend on the program's being part of a particular software distribution. If the program is extracted from that distribution and used or distributed within the terms of the program's license, all parties to whom the program is redistributed should have the same rights as those that are granted in conjunction with the original software distribution.

9. License Must Not Contaminate Other Software

The license must not place restrictions on other software that is distributed along with the licensed software. For example, the license must not insist that all other programs distributed on the same medium must be open-source software.

The first ensures that the terms of an OSS license cannot be limited to a particular distribution or product. In other words, you cannot create software which is only open when part of a Red Hat Linux distribution, but suddenly becomes closed when found in a Caldera Linux distribution. This kind of licensing would effectively negate the first criterion of open redistribution. The other ensures that no requirements are made regarding other software co-located on the distribution medium. You cannot prohibit, for example, bundling the OSD-compliant Apache HTTP Server with a trial-version of the proprietary web development environment, Dreamweaver.

Examples of OSD-compliant licenses

As noted above, the Open Source Initiative (2001a) provides a list of licenses that have been reviewed and found to be compliant with the OSD. At the time of writing, there were 21 licenses on the list, namely

- The GNU General Public License (GPL)

- The GNU Lesser Public License (LGPL)

- The Berkeley Software Distribution (BSD) License

- The MIT License

- The Artistic License

- The Mozilla Public License v. 1.0 and 1.1 (MPL 1.0 and MPL 1.1)

- The Qt Public License (QPL)

- The IBM Public License

- The MITRE Collaborative Virtual Workspace License (CVW License)

- The Ricoh Source Code Public License

- The Python License

- The zlib/libpng License

- The Apache Software License

- The Vovida Software License v. 1.0

- The Sun Internet Standards Source License (SISSL)

- The Intel Open Source License

- The Jabber Open Source License

- The Nokia Open Source License

- The Sleepycat License

- The Nethack General Public License

Since all of these licenses conform to the OSD, we'll limit our comments to the more distinctive qualities of the most widely used licenses. The GPL and LGPL were created by Richard Stallman's Free Software Foundation (FSF) and, in fact, predate the coining of the term Open Source (see Chapter 2). There is an enormous amount of GPL-licensed software in circulation – 11,723 independent projects hosted at the SourceForge website alone[4] – and the FSF itself has

---

[4] http://sourceforge.net/softwaremap/trove_list.php?form_cat=14, accessed August 8, 2001.

produced over 170 mature products, collectively referred to as the GNU Project. GNU Project software includes the extremely popular Bash (Bourne Again SHell) shell environment, the multi-purpose Emacs editing environment, and GCC, one of the most widely used compiler collections for C/C++. Some notable GPL-licensed software produced outside of the FSF include the Linux kernel itself, the CVS version control system used by many Open Source projects, the Lynx web browser, Samba (for heterogeneous network integration), and the Perl programming language. Note that Perl carries a disjunctive license – users choose whether to use the GPL or Perl creator Larry Wall's Artistic License, which is closer in substance to the LGPL (see below).

> The Bourne Again Shell was so named because the author of the original shell was named Bourne, and thus, the natural name for a clone would of course be "Bourne again," proof that hackers have a well-honed sense of humor.

The most notable quality of the GPL is its "viral" nature. Users may modify GPL software in any way they see fit. However, if a modified version is publicly released, it must be distributed under the terms of the GPL. The FSF created a second license, the LGPL, to provide a non-viral alternative to the GPL. The LGPL was designed for use with programming language libraries. A library (sometimes called a module) is not a standalone application; rather it is a collection of routines that other applications can use. The LGPL states that if a program does not contain code derived from the library, but instead only links to the library, then that program is not covered by the LGPL. For example, *Developer A* writes a library containing routines for querying a database, called "runQuery," and releases it under the LGPL. If *Developer B* takes that code and extends it, the new code is also under the LGPL. If *Developer B* writes an entirely separate program that merely calls or links to the "runQuery" routine in the LGPL library, then the LGPL does not affect the new code. It should be noted that Richard Stallman (1999c) *strongly* encourages the use of the GPL rather than the LGPL, for decidedly political reasons. He states:

> Proprietary software developers have the advantage of money; free
> software developers need to make advantages for each other. Using the

ordinary GPL for a library gives free software developers an advantage over proprietary developers: a library that they can use, while proprietary developers cannot use it. Using the ordinary GPL is not advantageous ... when a free library's features are readily available for proprietary software through other alternative libraries. In that case, the library cannot give free software any particular advantage, so it is better to use the Library GPL for that library. ... However, when a library provides a significant unique capability, like GNU Readline, that's a horse of a different color. ... Releasing it under the GPL and limiting its use to free programs gives our community a real boost. At least one application program is free software today specifically because that was necessary for using Readline.

The BSD License and MIT License are also widely used; for example, there are 1,228 BSD and MIT licensed projects hosted by SourceForge.[5] The BSD License is pretty much at the opposite end of the scale from the GPL, and makes very few demands on the terms of distribution for modified versions of the software. These are:

- Redistributions of source code must retain the original copyright notice, list of conditions and the disclaimer of warranty.

- Redistributions in binary form must reproduce the original copyright notice, list of conditions, and the disclaimer of warranty in the documentation and/or other materials provided with the distribution.

- Neither the name of the original authors nor the names of subsequent contributors may be used to endorse or promote products derived from the software.

As a result of this permissiveness, we actually see chunks of BSD code used in Solaris, the Linux kernel, Windows NT, and Mac OS X (Rosenberg, 2000). The MIT License, originally developed to cover the X Window graphics system, is likewise quite loose, requiring

---

[5] http://sourceforge.net/softwaremap/trove_list.php?form_cat=14, accessed August 8, 2001.

only that the copyright notice and permission notice remain intact on full or substantial copies of the software.

Finally, Netscape's Mozilla Public License is starting to gain wider use. Netscape released the source code for Communicator 5.0 Standard Edition under two licenses, the Netscape Public License, which is much more restrictive to protect Netscape's interests and is not OSI approved, and the MPL, which is fully approved and considered more suitable for general use. The NPL and MPL, like other corporate licenses (IBM, Intel, Nokia, Sun, etc.), contain rather legalistic language and are different in tone from the "community-bred" licenses like the GPL and BSD. The MPL is important for another reason as well as Netscape was the first large proprietary company to adopt the OSS licensing approach.

The remaining licenses tend to be limited in use to their namesake products or companies, although the Python License is becoming more popular. The Apache Software License is not too widely used outside of the Apache Software Foundation (see Chapter 3), but the prolific nature of that organization means there is a large body of Apache licensed software in circulation anyway.

Table 1.1 lists the licenses and their web addresses.

Examples of Open Source Software products

In Chapter 5 we look at a few large collections of OSS products and discuss in detail the categorical trends and other structural characteristics that they share. In this section, we simply seek to familiarize the reader with some of the more popular and/or influential OSS products.

The Open Source community boasts two powerful operating systems. The more popular is **_Linux_**, which is also the fastest-growing operating system in the server market and second only to Windows NT for market share (Shankland, 2001). The Linux kernel was originally created by Linus Torvalds (see Chapter 2) and the bulk of the higher-level functionality in a Linux distribution is based on GNU Project software. For this reason, Linux is sometimes referred to as GNU/Linux. *FreeBSD* is the most successful of the BSD operating systems, and is the most popular OSS operating system after Linux. In particular, FreeBSD has received wide acclaim for its network performance and robust security, and is, for example, the operating system used to run the Yahoo! web portal.

Like all flavors of Unix, Linux and BSD are often billed as esoteric and hard to use. Fortunately, there are two richly featured Open Source graphical desktop environments available, *GNOME* and *KDE*, which work in conjunction with the Open Source *X Windows* system. The GNOME and KDE projects are both also working on OSS office suites, *KOffice* and *GNOME Office* respectively. Sun Microsystems is also developing an OSS office suite, *OpenOffice*.

One of the most widely used OSS products is the *Apache HTTP Server* – the web server currently running over 60 percent of the world's websites (Netcraft, 2001a). Like FreeBSD, Apache is known for its enormous stability. In Netcraft's (2001b) list of the top 50

TABLE 1.1 OSI-approved licenses

Licenses	URL
Artistic License	http://www.perl.com/pub/language/misc/Artistic.html
GNU General Public License (GPL)	http://www.fsf.org/copyleft/gpl.html
GNU Lesser Public License (LGPL)	http://www.fsf.org/copyleft/lesser.html
Berkeley Software Distribution (BSD) License	http://www.opensource.org/licenses/bsd-license.html
MIT License	http://www.opensource.org/licenses/mit-license.html
Mozilla Public License	http://www.mozilla.org/MPL/MPL-1.1.html
Python License	http://www.opensource.org/licenses/pythonpl.html and http://www.python.org/doc/Copyright.html
Apache Software License	http://www.apache.org/LICENSE-1.1.txt

sites with highest average uptime in the previous 90 days, only 4 out of the 50 sites were not running Apache (and only 6 were not running some form of BSD).

In addition to Apache, there are two other category-killing OSS Internet applications. The first is **Sendmail**, one of the most widely used Internet Mail Transport Agents, and the other is the Berkeley Internet Name Daemon (**BIND**), a Domain Name Server used to resolve domain names into Internet Protocol (IP) addresses, and vice versa. On the client side of Internet technologies, popular OSS products include the **Mozilla**, **Lynx**, and **Amaya** web browsers, and the **Pine** email client.

Perl is probably the most well-known OSS programming language. Perl has achieved its renown as a powerful tool for Unix system administration and as the *lingua franca* of Common Gateway Interface (CGI) programming for the web. The C programming language remains the most common one for building OSS applications (see Chapter 5), due in part to the GPL-licensed **GCC** compiler. Finally, **Python**, **TCL/TK**, and **PHP**, all OSS languages, are growing rapidly. Another prominent OSS development tool is the **Emacs** text editor, a multi-mode, multi-buffer, multi-purpose working environment and probably the best-known GNU application besides GCC.

The products mentioned in this section are listed in Table 1.2 with their web addresses.

The Open Source Software development process

In Chapter 6 we provide a detailed discussion of the OSS development process. In this section, we will only briefly characterize that process. There is, of course, no single OSS development process, and different projects are often managed in radically different ways (cf. Nakakoji and Yamamoto, 2001). However, we can point to a number of characteristics that are found in the majority of OSS projects.

The OSS process generally involves (or has the potential to involve) *large, globally distributed communities of developers collaborating primarily through the Internet.* These developers tend to *work in parallel,* with different individuals/groups working on different aspects of the system simultaneously. OSS development communities often exploit the power of *peer review* to facilitate the debugging process, better articulate system requirements, and speed up the process of feature enhancement. OSS projects are generally characterized by *rapid, incremental release schedules,* in which limited extra functionality is added in each release. Proprietary software companies tend to follow the opposite model, introducing substantial change in software products but very infrequently. OSS, particularly the larger projects, has attracted a very large pool of *experienced and esteemed professional developers.* Furthermore, the

TABLE 1.2 Major OSS products

Products	URL
Linux	http://www.kernel.org
FreeBSD	http://www.freebsd.org
GNOME	http://www.gnome.org
KDE	http://www.kde.org
X Windows	http://www.x.org
Koffice	http://www.koffice.org
GNOME Office	http://www.gnome.org/gnome-office/
OpenOffice	http://www.openoffice.org
Apache HTTP Server	http://httpd.apache.org
Sendmail	http://sendmail.net
BIND	http://www.isc.org/products/BIND/
Mozilla	http://www.mozilla.org
Lynx	http://lynx.isc.org
Amaya	http://www.w3.org/Amaya/
Pine	http://www.washington.edu/pine/
Perl	http://www.perl.com
GCC	http://www.gnu.org/software/gcc/gcc.html
Python	http://www.python.org
TCL/TK	http://www.scriptics.com/software/
PHP	http://www.php.net/
Emacs	http://www.gnu.org/software/emacs/emacs.html

self-selected, volunteer nature of OSS has meant that projects have been coordinated and supported by *highly motivated* communities. OSS user communities tend to be highly active, and contribute by articulating requirements, testing functionality, reporting bugs, writing documentation, etc.

Conclusion

In this chapter we have provided a basic overview of Open Source Software. OSS is defined as software which can be obtained in source code as well as binary form; can be freely redistributed, for free or for profit, modified or unmodified; can be freely used without discrimination against persons, groups, or fields of endeavor; which protects the integrity of the original authors' code and ensures the same rights extend to all users; which is not limited to a specific product or distribution of products, and does not seek to affect the licensing terms of software collocated on the distribution medium. These criteria are formally articulated in the Open Source Definition, which is maintained as a certification standard by the Open Source Initiative. There are a number of OSI certified licenses, the most prominent of which are the GPL/LGPL, BSD, and MIT Licenses. There is an enormous amount of Open Source software in circulation. However, only a handful of products have attracted significant mainstream attention, notably Linux, Apache, Sendmail, BIND, Mozilla, and Perl. The OSS development process, although not homogeneous, can be briefly characterized as consisting of distributed, parallel development supported by rapid release cycles and communication methods, and collaboration among highly talented and motivated developers and users. In the next chapter, we discuss the history of the OSS movement

2

A history of Open Source Software

In this chapter we provide a brief historical account of OSS, from the earliest traditions of code sharing through the establishment of the Free Software Foundation to the contemporary advocacy campaign of the Open Source Initiative.

The early days

In the early years of computing, during the 1940s, the computer was primarily used for scientific problem solving. It was needed principally because of its speed of mathematical calculation and was applied in areas such as the calculation of missile trajectories, aerodynamics, and seismic data analysis. The users of computers at the time were typically scientists with a strong mathematical or engineering background who developed their own programs to address the particular areas in which they were carrying out research. For example, one of the early computers, ENIAC (Electronic Numerical Integrator and Calculator), which was operational in the ten-year period 1945–55, is reckoned to have done more arithmetic than had been done by the whole human race prior to 1945. In this type of environment, the concept of commercial software was alien, and software was shared freely.

During the early 1950s, the use of computers began to spread beyond that of scientific problem solving to address the area of business data processing. These early data processing applications were concerned with the complete and accurate capture of the organization's business transactions, and with automating routine clerical tasks to make them quicker and more accurate. The nature of business data processing was very different from the computation-intensive nature of scientific applications. Business applications involve high volumes of input and output, but the input and output peripherals at the time were very slow and inefficient. Also, memory capacity was very limited, and this led to the widespread conviction among developers that good programs were efficient programs, rather than clear, well-documented, and easily understood programs.

Given these problems, writing programs required much creativity and resourcefulness on the part of the programmer. Indeed, it was recognized that it was a major achievement to get a program to run at all in the 1950s. Thus, if software worked it was shared widely. An early formalized example of this free sharing of software was the PACT (Project for Advancement of Coding Techniques) initiative, established in 1953 as a collaboration between military and aviation industries, who were actually in competition with each other (Leonard, 2000). The motivation for the collaboration, interestingly, was instigated by the programmers who then persuaded management of the efficiency benefits. Thus, the principal rationale behind the PACT initiative was one of efficiency, rather than any idealistic or altruistic underpinning ideology. Other examples of free sharing of source code at the time involved user groups at IBM and DEC, and also the *Algorithms* section of the *Communications of the ACM* (Barahona *et al.*, 1999).

This trend of software development for business quickly spread, and by 1960, the business data processing use of computers had overtaken the scientific one. Once under way, the business use of computers accelerated at an extremely rapid rate, evidenced by the fact that in the US, the number of computer installations increased more than twenty-fold between 1960 and 1970 (Lecht, 1977).

Another significant event of this era which helped ensure the availability of free software was the 1956 US government consent decree which forbade the telecommunications giant, AT&T, from entering non-telephony markets such as computing (Leonard, 2000).

This effectively ensured that the Unix operating system, which was developed at AT&T Bell Labs in 1969 by Dennis Ritchie and Ken Thompson, could not be sold commercially. The story goes that Thompson wanted to play a favorite computer game, Space Travel, on a PDP-7 computer, and wrote an entire operating system to accomplish this. At any rate, given that AT&T were prohibited from exploiting Unix commercially, it was distributed with the actual source code to universities and other research institutions for a nominal fee. Again, there was no grand plan or ideology at the heart of the original 1956 consent decree – no one at the time foresaw that the convergence of telecommunications and computing would be such a critical industry sector by the end of the twentieth century.

> Such stories of stupendous feats of coding to satisfy personal whims abound in the computing field. For example, legend has it that the Apple computer was developed by Steve Wozniak to allow him play his favorite computer game (Breakout) in color.

The Berkeley Software Distribution

One of the most effective and well-known distribution channels for Unix and related software was the Berkeley Software Distribution (BSD), established in 1977 at the University of California at Berkeley. The BSD project was headed by Bill Joy, who later went on to co-found Sun Microsystems. The BSD group modified and improved the Unix system and redistributed it to others who in turn contributed their own enhancements, thus making BSD Unix even more powerful. It even became the choice of DARPA (Defense Advanced Research Projects Agency) for linking together the Arpanet research nodes that later became the Internet (Leonard, 2000). The BSD group also developed a TCP/IP protocol suite which was widely disseminated and which also contributed enormously to the rapid diffusion of the Internet. Other important Internet utilities that were developed as part of the BSD were Sendmail and BIND. Sendmail was developed initially by Eric Allman to facilitate the routing of mail messages to individuals who had multiple mail addresses on different machines. It is currently estimated to be the mail agent for 80 percent of all Internet email traffic. The BIND utility implements the Domain Name Server (DNS) which maps domain names to actual IP addresses, for example, **http:// opensource.ucc.ie** to 143.239.93.204. BIND is reckoned to be the most mission-critical software underpinning the whole Internet.

There have been many phases in the BSD Unix history. In 1984, following the break-up of their monopoly, AT&T sought to commercialize Unix. An acrimonious court battle with BSD over copyright violation resulted in claims and counter-claims by both sides, and was eventually resolved in the early 1990s, but the uncertainty of the outcome of the court battle with AT&T ensured that many volunteer developers opted for contributing to the Linux project, protected as it was by the GNU General Public License (more about both later). Also, the BSD project forked into several competing offerings, FreeBSD, OpenBSD, and NetBSD. Although each had slightly different objectives, this forking nevertheless served to dilute the BSD effort.

An important aspect of the BSD initiative is that it marked the beginning of a more ideological underpinning in the free software history; for example, BSD software was not available in South Africa during the apartheid regime. This stands in contrast to the improved efficiency motivation that lay behind previous initiatives in the free sharing of software.

T_eX

Donald Knuth is one of the true giants in the history of the computing field. His multi-volume work, *The Art of Computer Programming*,[1] is reckoned to be the most famous computer science

---

[1] Knuth took early retirement to give him more time to complete all the work he wanted to finish. He is currently working on Volume 4 of *The Art of Computer Programming*, popularly known as TAOCP.

book. Knuth is an important figure in the history of free software – he has spent a lifetime sharing his work in his writings and in the production of actual software solutions. In true Open Source spirit, he issues calls for help with suggestions for his books, even down to the rather eccentric task of completing the full names of all those cited in his books – some citations do not contain the complete set of first names. (He does *pay* \$2.56 (i.e. 2^8 cents) for every name completed. In keeping with this spirit, we offer here Eric Steven Raymond and Linus Benedict Torvalds.)

One of Knuth's major contributions to free software was T_eX, the ubiquitous typesetting system that is used throughout the world; indeed, it is estimated that T_eX is used for typesetting more than 90 percent of the books published in mathematics and physics. The story goes that Knuth was frustrated at the decline in print quality and opted to write a complete typesetting system himself to address the problem. T_eX was one of the first big free software projects where the software source code was published openly, and it has been very useful in this regard. Recently, an Australian research group has begun a project, the Omega Typesetting System,[2] whose goal is to extend T_eX to print all the world's languages, past or present, regardless of how widespread or rare they are.

Knuth has won many accolades and has been nominated by the Free Software Foundation for an award, and in an ironic twist, is also a hero to Bill Gates, who described his reading of *The Art of Computer Programming* as follows:

> It took incredible discipline, and several months, for me to read it. I studied 20 pages, put it away for a week, and came back for another 20 pages. If somebody is so brash that they think they know everything, Knuth will help them understand that the world is deep and complicated. If you can read the whole thing, send me a resumé.

---

[2] http://www.serg.cse.unsw.edu.au/DoSE/research.html

The Free Software Foundation

One of the most significant milestones in the history of OSS was the establishment of the Free Software Foundation (FSF) by Richard Stallman in 1985. The idealism underpinning the FSF was (and continues to be) particularly strong. The story goes that while working at the Artificial Intelligence Laboratory at MIT in 1979, Stallman's group received the first laser printer from Xerox. The printer used to jam on occasions, and would then require some human intervention to rectify the problem. Stallman requested the driver source code from Xerox with the intention of modifying it to provide an alert when the printer required intervention – the traditional solution to such problems in the AI Laboratory. However, Xerox refused to provide the source code. Ironically, Stallman has since apparently admitted that if Xerox had provided the code under a non-disclosure agreement he would have been satisfied, but the Xerox rejection caused him to move to a fundamental belief that software should be free. Prophetically, he foresaw a scenario whereby a monopoly could arise through the closed software model.

Stallman resigned from MIT and devoted his attention to creating a suite of free software products, the GNU family. In the GNU manifesto, Stallman (1985) coined the term "Free Software," thus formalizing a process that had been going on in a relatively *ad hoc* fashion in the past. However, the ambiguity of the word "free," having both the meaning "unfettered" and also "*gratis,*" led to the eventual coining of the term "Open Source" later. As previously noted, the FSF has been responsible for a number of very widely used utilities which are at the heart of many of the later OSS products, the GNU C compiler (GCC) and the Emacs editor being two of the best-known and most widely used examples.

The strong ideological nature of the FSF – evident in the terms of the licenses associated with it – is typified by the recasting of the common copyright phrase, *copyright – all rights reserved,* to be '*copyleft – all rights reversed*'. Under the copyleft concept, everyone could have permission to run the software, copy or modify it, even redistribute it, but they could not add any restrictions of their own.

A more contentious aspect of the GPL – as discussed in Chapter 1 – is the requirement that if a software product's code is derived from code covered by the GPL, then that software must also be covered by the GPL – termed a viral license for that reason.

Linux

In 1991, Linus Torvalds, a 21-year-old Helsinki university student, began what has become the poster child of OSS – the Linux operating system. Torvalds modeled his system on Minix, a Unix clone developed by Andrew Tanenbaum at the Free University in Amsterdam. Minix was available in source code form, although any modifications to the source code required Tanenbaum's permission. Minix had itself been very popular, with a newsgroup of more than 40,000 users worldwide, according to Tanenbaum.

Torvalds' objective with Linux was to create a Unix-like operating system for the IBM PC 386 series, and he openly sought help with the project. Interestingly, Torvalds' original choice of name for the system was Freax, a conflation of the terms "free," "freak," and an "x" as a final letter in keeping with the prevailing nomenclature for operating systems. However, he was persuaded to adopt the name Linux instead by Ari Lemke at the Helsinki University of Technology who was one of the first to read his call-for-help message, and offered a sub-directory on the university's ftp site for the system when it became available. Torvalds succeeded in attracting a great deal of support worldwide. Estimates suggest that more than a thousand developers have

It's worth noting that the viral nature of the GPL is still a hot topic of discussion, particularly in the Free Software Business mailing list (archives at http://apocalypse.org/pub/fsb/) where it has been insightfully noted by Stephen J. Turnbull that the "GPL doesn't 'force' you to GPL *your* software, it prohibits you from using the GPL-licensed software if you don't. Carrot, not stick." (June 24, 2001, quoted with permission).

Whatever about Linux being a poster child, Linus Torvalds is very frank about his own limitations in that respect. He opens his wonderful account of the development of Linux (*Just for Fun: The Story of an Accidental Revolutionary*, Torvalds and Diamond, 2001) with the phrase, "I was an ugly child." The book continues in that refreshing vein, and early on he states that "the traditional oversized Torvalds nose" limited his options in relation to other diversions that might have distracted him from programming. One is reminded of Blaise Pascal's remark, "Cleopatra's nose, had it been shorter, the whole face of the world would have been changed," and can merely speculate as to whether the face of software and indeed the world would have been otherwise if the reverse applied to Linus Torvalds.

collaborated on the Linux kernel development alone, while on the overall Linux operating system, the worldwide development community is estimated to exceed 40,000[3] developers (Raymond, 2001CatB), or even "hundreds of thousands of developers" and a user base of 25 million (Torvalds and Diamond, 2001). Whatever about the estimates, Torvalds claims, with uncharacteristic immodesty, that it represents the largest collaborative project in the history of the world.

Ironically, Linux has become more popular than Unix, the operating system on which it was initially based. It is currently the most widely ported operating system available on the PC platform. Also, several major players in the computing industry, such as Computer Associates, Corel, IBM, Oracle, and Sun Microsystems, have committed to providing their products on a Linux platform. As noted previously, at the end of 2000, Linux accounted for 27 percent of the enterprise server market (Shankland, 2001). Furthermore, a survey carried out by the IDC group predicts that its market share will grow faster than all other operating systems combined through 2003 (Raymond, 2001MC).

While Linux has moved to a position of pre-eminence, assumed by many to be synonymous with Open Source Software, it should be borne in mind that a typical Linux distribution is heavily dependent on utilities and tools that were developed by both the BSD and FSF movements (in fact the bulk of a Linux distribution is outside of the kernel). Indeed, Richard Stallman (1999a) refers to it as the GNU/Linux operating system and categorizes it as Free Software.

Apache

The next milestone in the history of OSS was the development of the Apache[4] HTTP Server, begun in February 1995 by a group of

---

[3] The basis for arriving at this figure is not provided. McConnell (1999) suggests that 1,200 programmers have contributed to Linux development – still an exceptionally high figure for a voluntary initiative.
[4] The name arises from the phrase "a patchy server."

volunteers who decided to pool expertise rather than duplicate work by reinventing the wheel in isolation (Fielding, 1999). The Apache Server was based on a series of patches to the web server initially developed by Rob McCool at the National Center for Supercomputing Applications (NCSA). The NCSA web server had been popular and many individual webmasters had developed extensions or patches, but the NCSA had ceased development work when a key individual left (to form Netscape), and so this work was in something of a limbo in terms of the distribution and incorporation of these patches. A group of volunteers came together to coordinate the distribution of these patches, and Brian Behlendorf provided a server to host the project.

There are currently 33 members in the "Apache Core Group" (Apache Software Foundation, 2000). These volunteers are invited to participate, based on their active contribution to the project. All modifications to the Apache Server are voted on by the group, and a constitution for the group and its working protocols have been explicitly formalized (Apache Software Foundation, 2001b). Plans for development and proposed changes are maintained in the source repositories. This helps ensure that contributors do not duplicate the work of others, vital given that core developers are located in the US, Britain, Canada, Germany, and Italy (Fielding, 1999). The resulting end product has been a phenomenal success, as noted previously. Further confirmation of its pre-eminence was achieved when IBM joined the project in 1998 and ported it to the AS400 platform. The most significant contribution of IBM's involvement, however, was the huge boost that it gave to the commercial credibility of the OSS movement. The Apache Group became the Apache Software Foundation in 1999, and the HTTP Server project is only one of many Foundation projects active today (see Chapter 3).

Mozilla

One of the most important initiatives in the history of Open Source Software is the Mozilla Project; in addition to the software that it has produced, it had an enormous impact in promoting corporate and media awareness of the concept. In January 1998, Netscape announced that the source code for their browser would be made available, and Mozilla was the name chosen for the project. Prior to "Freeing the Lizard," as some have phrased it, Netscape were at 13 percent of market share with their Navigator browser and losing ground rapidly to Microsoft's Internet Explorer. Faced with this serious threat to their very survival, Netscape took the extremely courageous and hitherto unprecedented step of making the source code of their browser available.[5] However, the OSS ideal was very much alien to the tradition of most software companies who distributed their software only as binary executables, preserving strict privacy over the actual source code. Netscape admitted publicly to having been influenced by Raymond's (2001CatB) classic paper, *The Cathedral and the Bazaar*, which discussed the Open Source concept, and Raymond (along with Bruce Perens, Richard Stallman, and others) were invited to discuss the issue with the group that initiated the Mozilla strategy within Netscape. Raymond (2001RotH) saw the Mozilla Project as an opportunity to spread the OSS message to the wider business community, but recognized the high risk to the overall credibility of OSS if the project were to fail.

> For those interested in such things (we are), Mozilla was the internal code name for the Navigator browser at Netscape – the rationale being that the group were trying to create a "beast" more powerful than the Mosaic browser at NCSA, whence the Netscape founders had emanated.

Netscape formed a group, The Mozilla Organization, to act as a central coordinator for work on the project. An owner is designated for each module, with responsibility for incorporating contributions to the project. A special pair of licenses, the Mozilla Public License (MPL) and the Netscape Public License (NPL), were created for the project. The MPL is an OSI-certified, fairly generic OSS license. As noted previously, the NPL is not OSI-certified, and contains specific

---

[5] One could of course argue that since Netscape's origins were in the Open Source environment of the University of Illinois, it was only fair that the product should revert to Open Source status.

clauses which allow Netscape (and only Netscape) to re-license third-party Mozilla developments to create a proprietary product.

This business strategy appeared to work, initially at any rate, for Netscape. Within hours of the source code being made available on March 25, 1998, developers around the world were submitting patches to code. While Netscape provided most of the resources to run the project initially, they received many contributions, including patches to allow porting to new platforms and an XML parser. Also, in December 1998, the Gecko product for rendering web pages was released. This was principally developed under the auspices of the Mozilla Project (Hecker, 1999). By the end of 1998, the company was starting to regain market share. Also, following the takeover of Netscape by America Online, there has been a public commitment to the Mozilla project.

Initially, the success of the Mozilla Project was questioned by observers (such as Elgin, 1998), who suggested that the project was little more than hype, citing the fact that the Mozilla mailing list declined by 58 percent between April and June 1998 (Lewis, 1999). Also, the public resignation of one of the lead developers on the project, Jamie Zawinski, due to apparent frustrations with the management of the project and the failure to exploit opportunities, did not help the public perception of the project. However, the Mozilla Project has been phenomenally prolific. In addition to Mozilla and Netscape 6.x, the Beonex, IBM Web Browser for OS/2, Aphrodite, Q.BATi, Galeon, Skipstone, and K-Meleon projects are all based on the Mozilla Gecko layout engine. The Mozilla Project is also developing an HTML 4.0-compliant WYSIWYG editor, Instant Messaging and chat utilities, Java integration tools, C and Java implementations of JavaScript (ECMAScript), and implementations of the W3C's Mathematical Markup Language, P3P, Scalable Vector Graphics Language, XSL Transformations (XSLT), and Resource Description Framework (RDF) specifications. Mozilla also includes several projects related to security, such as Network Security Services (NSS), Network Security Services for Java (JSS), Personal Security Manager (PSM), and Component Security. The list goes on

– there are dozens of other projects under way within Mozilla.org, and as many or more third-party projects based on Mozilla technology.

Open Source Software

Following his participation in the initiation of the Mozilla strategy, Raymond discussed the need for a long-term strategy in relation to bringing Free Software to a wider audience with a number of interested individuals, and on February 3, 1998, "Open Source" was coined as an alterative term. One of those involved in the decision was Bruce Perens who had produced the *Debian Free Software Guidelines*[6] for the Debian project – a Linux distribution that included only GPL-licensed software. The founding of the Open Source Initiative was an extension of this activity.

The group was conscious of the fact that a predominant interpretation of "free" was that it meant "no cost" or *gratis*, which ensured that it was seen as anti-commercial among the business community. Further contributing to this anti-commercial perception was the zealous anti-commercial spirit that became associated with the Free Software movement, which was not helped by the fact that the FSF was launched on the basis of a "manifesto" – a term that was sure to engender suspicion among the business community. In Perens' words, the Open Source advocates wanted to "market the free software concept to the people who wore suits" (Perens, 1999). The FSF, of course, never intended the word "free" to refer to cost. Indeed, the FSF itself *sells* GNU software on CD-ROM.

The key product of the Open Source Initiative[7] is the Open Source Definition (discussed in Chapter 1 and again in Chapter 5), which, as noted previously, was based on Perens' *Debian Free Software Guidelines*.[8] In October of 1998, the OSI received an early

---

[6] http://www.debian.org/social_contract#guidelines
[7] http://www.opensource.org
[8] Perens has since left the OSI. See Chapter 10.

Christmas present, in the form of the so-called "Halloween Documents," a set of confidential internal Microsoft memos leaked to the OSS community. The Halloween Documents (1998) discuss the concerns of Microsoft and the threat posed by OSS in general and Linux in particular. The memos caused a huge increase in media interest in the Open Source topic, thus satisfying one of the primary objectives of the Open Source group: in Raymond's (2001RotH) words, "Wall Street, finally, came to us."

Conclusion and further reading

In this chapter we have provided a brief history of OSS. From the earliest days of computing, an ethos of code sharing predominated. This culture of collaboration continued to exist underground even after the rise of a proprietary software industry. In the mid-1980s the practice of sharing code, and granting software users the freedom to use the code as they saw fit, was formalized in the work of Richard Stallman and the Free Software Foundation. The early 1990s saw the emergence of two products that would later become the poster children of OSS – Linux and Apache. By the close of the century, many of the leaders within the Free Software movement (notably, *not* Stallman) adopted the term Open Source Software as the first step in a campaign to bring Free Software to the mainstream. To this end, the Open Source Initiative was created, and celebrated its first significant success with the opening of Netscape's browser.

By necessity, this history has been rather short. Readers interested in greater detail may find the following sources useful:

▶

- *Rebel Code* by Glyn Moody (London: Penguin Press, 2001)
- *Free for All* by Peter Wayner (New York: Harper Business, 2000)
- "A Brief History of Hackerdom" (Raymond, 2001BHH)
- *Open Sources* (DiBona *et al.*, 1999)
- *Salon Free Software Project* (Leonard, 2000).

3

The landscape of Open Source Software

In this chapter we discuss the current activities of some of the major organizations and companies involved in Open Source Software. Specifically, we examine two OSS advocacy groups, the FSF and OSI. We also consider various OSS project coordinators and hosts, such as the Apache Software Foundation (ASF), the Linux Kernel Archives, the GNOME Foundation, the Perl Porters Group, and the Open Source Development Network (OSDN). Finally, we identify a number of OSS companies, both "pure-play" and hybrid, and some related OSS organizations.

Advocacy groups – FSF and OSI

In Chapter 2 we discussed the historical events leading to the formation of the Free Software Foundation (FSF) and, later, the Open Source Initiative (OSI). Here, we look at what these two advocacy groups are doing today.

Although both organizations want ultimately the same thing – the proliferation of quality software that can be freely obtained, copied, modified, and redistributed – there is considerable philosophical contestation between the FSF and the OSI. The FSF is fundamentally motivated by an *ethical* position focused on the freedoms associated with software, while the OSI has taken a *pragmatic* position focused on the superiority of software produced in an Open Source fashion. This conflict is symbolized by a long-standing disagreement over the terms used by the organizations, namely Free Software (FS) vs. Open Source.

In June of 1999, Richard Stallman (1999b) posted a message to the Slashdot bulletin board stating:

> People have been speaking of me in the context of the Open Source movement. That's misleading because I am not a member of it. I belong to the Free Software movement. In this movement we talk about freedom, about principle, about the rights that computer users are entitled to. The Open Source movement avoids talking about those issues, and that is why I am not joining it. The two movements can work together on software … But we disagree on the basic issues. …

Elsewhere, Stallman (1998) had already written a lengthy essay on these "basic issues," arguing that while replacing the term "Free" with "Open Source" solved some problems, it created other, more serious ones. This earlier essay concludes by saying that the two movements are like competing political parties. Stallman writes:

> Radical groups are known for factionalism … They agree on the basic principles, and disagree only on practical recommendations … For the Free Software movement and the Open Source movement, it is just the opposite … We disagree on the basic principles, but agree on most practical recommendations … In the Free Software movement, we don't think of the Open Source movement as an enemy. The enemy is proprietary software. But we do want people in our community to know that we are not the same as them!

Eric Raymond, who had been specifically named in Stallman's Slashdot posting, responded on the same day with an essay provocatively entitled "Shut up and show them the code" (Raymond, 1999). In his response, Raymond says that Stallman is right, the Open Source movement does avoid talking about "freedom, about principle, about the rights that computer users are entitled to." However, he argues that this is the case, not because the OSI disagrees with these ideas, but because doing so "is ineffective, is bad tactics." In direct contradiction of Stallman's earlier (1998) essay, Raymond states that the real disagreement between the OSI and FSF is over "tactics and rhetoric." Raymond goes on to justify the OSI's approach by citing the enormous shift in mainstream perception and corporate buy-in that resulted from the OSI's initial (and continuing) public campaign. Raymond concludes:

> OSI's tactics work. … the FSF's tactics don't work, and never did. … RMS's best propaganda has always been his hacking. So it is for all of us; to the rest of the world outside our little tribe, the excellence of our software is a far more persuasive argument for openness and freedom than any amount of highfalutin appeal to abstract principles. So the next time RMS, or anybody else, urges you to "talk about freedom", I urge you to reply "Shut up and show them the code."

Despite its bloodsport-like mass appeal, the more public expressions of this debate disappeared quickly, and both organizations returned their focus to taking care of business as usual.

For the FSF, "business as usual" means three things. First, it involves maintaining and watch-dogging the Free Software Definition (Free Software Foundation, 1996), a document analogous, and substantively identical, to the OSD. The FSF has applied this definition to a large, thorough, and regularly updated list of software licenses (Stallman, 2001a). Second, the FSF (more accurately, Stallman) has published over a hundred essays (plus translations) on Free Software, copyright, patents, and related issues.[1] Finally, the FSF oversees the ongoing GNU Software Project. The goal of the GNU Project is to develop an entirely free Unix-like operating system, and at this point, the project is nearly complete. The one remaining component to be developed is the actual OS kernel (the GNU Hurd), although there is little pressure for the Hurd to ever be released, since the rest of the GNU system is widely and successfully used with the Linux kernel (which is also under the GPL).

---

[1] http://www.fsf.org/philosophy

The OSI also maintains a software licensing specification (namely, the Open Source Definition), although as previously discussed, the OSI has gone one step further than the FSF and formalized their control over the specification by registering the legally protected *OSI Certified* mark. The similarity between the two groups ends there and, in terms of daily operation, the OSI leads a substantially different life indeed. The FSF have focused on the production of GNU software and on internal publications. The OSI, on the other hand, do not produce any software and have focused their time and efforts on a very large, very aggressive marketing campaign, courting (quite successfully) the mind share of mainstream media groups and the strategic and management communities. This media campaign is described in detail in Raymond's (2001RotH) essay, *Revenge of the Hackers*.

Despite differences in tactics (as Raymond sees it) and/or principles (as Stallman sees it), in practice these two advocacy groups complement each other well. The FSF continues to fuel much of the FS/OSS development world, seeding the product base with the prolific GNU Project and inspiring individual developers with Stallman's thoughtful, if polemic, writings. The OSI supplements these activities by legitimating the FS/OSS movement in the eyes of the mainstream business community or, as Raymond put it, "the rest of the world outside our little tribe."

Project coordinators and hosts

Many small to medium-scale OSS projects are coordinated by a single individual or by a small, unofficial group. However, nearly all of the major OSS projects discussed in Chapter 1 are coordinated by official or quasi-official organizations (like the FSF's GNU Software Project described above).

One of the most prolific and influential OSS project coordinators is the Apache Software Foundation (ASF). As discussed in Chapter 2, the ASF is a not-for-profit corporation that came into existence in mid-1999, growing out of the Apache Group which was formed in 1995. The ASF is managed by a board of directors,[2] which is elected annually by the ASF membership. Like the Apache Server core group, membership in the ASF is by invitation only, and is generally only extended to individuals who have made significant contributions (in code, not cash) to the various ASF projects. New members must be nominated by an existing member, and then approved by a majority vote. Currently, the ASF consists of 62 members (Apache Software Foundation, 2001e), although it should be noted that this is *Foundation* membership – the various ASF projects include hundreds of participants. The day-to-day operations of the ASF are actually managed by a group of officers who are appointed by the board of directors. A self-selected team of active contributors to the project manages individual ASF projects. The ASF oversees many projects, including:

- The Apache HTTP Server Project (the hugely successful web server discussed previously);

- The Apache XML Project (various XML processing tools, also highly influential);

- Jakarta (an umbrella term for the ASF's Java activity – including Tomcat, the official reference implementation for the Java Servlet and JavaServer Pages technologies, which was named the "Most Innovative Java Product" of 2001 (Wilson, 2001));

- mod_perl (Apache HTTP Server/Perl integration);

- Apache Tcl (Apache HTTP Server/Tcl integration);

- PHP (a server-side HTML embedded scripting language, growing rapidly in popularity).

---

[2] Currently Brian Behlendorf, Ken Coar, Roy T. Fielding (chairman), Dirk-Willem van Gulik, Jim Jagielski, Ben Laurie, Greg Stein, Bill Stoddard, and Randy Terbush (Apache Software Foundation, 2001c)

The ongoing development of the Linux kernel is coordinated by Linus Torvalds, *not* by an official organization; however, an authoritative repository of kernel code can be found at The Linux Kernel Archives (hosted by Transmeta, Linus Torvalds' current employer). There are also two official organizations focused on creating desktop environments and productivity applications for OSS operating systems like Linux. The GNOME Foundation oversees the GNOME Project (which is officially part of the GNU Software Project discussed above) and The KDE Free Qt Foundation supports the KDE Project, in association with the Norwegian software company, Troll Tech. The GNOME and KDE projects are essentially identical in scope, and both foundations are focused on creating a windows-based graphical desktop development platform for these environments, and a suite of office productivity applications. As discussed in the previous chapter, the Mozilla Project is also an extremely active organization involved in a variety of projects in addition to the Mozilla browser.

There are three groups involved with coordinating the Perl programming language. The Perl language itself is maintained by the Perl Porters Group, an unofficial core-group that includes Perl creator Larry Wall. A separate group, called CPAN (Comprehensive Perl Archive Network), handles the archiving and distribution of both the Perl language and the hundreds of modules and scripts created by the global Perl development community. A third group, Perl Mongers, is a not-for-profit corporation focused on Perl advocacy. Likewise, the development and evolution of the Python programming language is coordinated by an official organization, namely the Python Software Foundation (a non-profit corporation patterned after the Apache Software Foundation).

Not all OSS projects are large enough to warrant an official organization, or even an independently maintained web presence. Many smaller OSS projects instead make use of free project hosting services. SourceForge, a part of the Open Source Development Network (OSDN), which is supported by VA Linux Systems, is by far and away the largest host, with over 20,000 OSS projects under one roof. SourceForge provides the coordinators of smaller OSS projects with a CVS repository, mailing lists and message forums, bug tracking tools, project management software, etc. and is open to any project using an OSI-certified license. Other OSDN sites include the Freshmeat OSS directory and the Slashdot discussion and news site, among others.

OSS companies

In Chapter 7, we examine the similarities and differences between OSS companies in greater detail. For present purposes, it is sufficient to divide OSS companies into two categories – pure-play companies which have a purely OSS business model, and hybrid companies which mix proprietary and OSS business models. Representative companies are discussed below.

Pure-play companies

- Red Hat is the most successful Linux distributor in the corporate market. Other pure-play commercial Linux distributors include Caldera, Suse, and Linux Mandrake. Most Linux distributors also provide training and support and do a certain amount of development.

- VA Linux is the most successful pure-play vendor of full Linux systems (although they have recently shifted their focus to software and services as previously noted). Other systems vendors include Penguin Computing and Atipa.

- Sleepycat Software provides support for Berkley DB, an OSS embedded database. Other companies that generate revenue purely from the support of existing products include Covalent (Apache HTTP Server), ActiveState (Perl, Python, and Tcl), and Riverace (ACE).

- Walnut Creek Software is a massive distributor of OSS products, similar to Linux Mall.

- Zelerate (formerly Open Sales) develops and supports an OSS e-commerce platform. Other companies developing specialist OSS products include Lutris Technologies and Ximian.

- Cosource hosts a many-to-many auction linking OSS developers with corporate users needing work done.

- CollabNet – until April 2001, CollabNet's SourceXchange service competed in the same space as Cosource. CollabNet is focused on enabling Open Source and collaborative development in corporate contexts.

Hybrid companies

- IBM has injected an enormous amount of money ($1billion in 2001) and code into OSS, has ported many of their products to Linux (they have 1,500 developers working on Linux), and uses Linux and Apache in its solution offerings.

- Apple Computers has released the core of Mac OS X under an OSS license and is moving towards open sourcing the QuickTime Streaming Server.

- SGI sponsors the Samba Project, has ported Linux to SGI/MIPS machines, and has open-sourced the XFS journaling file system.

- Netscape Communications really brought the OSS movement into the spotlight when it released Open Source versions of its client software (Netscape Communicator and Netscape Navigator).

- Corel Corporation offers a distribution of Linux in addition to its wide range of proprietary products.

- Dell, Gateway, and Compaq – three of the largest systems vendors now offer the option of factory-installed Linux. Cobalt (now owned by Sun Microsystems) is another key hybrid systems vendor.

- Sun Microsystems has likewise contributed both code and capital to the OSS community, and is behind notable OSS projects like NetBeans and OpenOffice.

Related organizations

There are several other organizations that deserve mention. First, there are two organizations attempting to "port" OSS concepts to areas other than software. The OpenContent movement has created an OSS-like license to cover non-executable content (the FSF has a similar license called the GNU Free Documentation License), and the Open Hardware Certification Program seeks to create a certification mark for hardware. Second, the technology publisher O'Reilly has established itself as one of the key patrons of the Open Source movement. Third and finally, the World Wide Web Consortium and the Internet Engineering Task Force are both active proponents, and producers, of Open Source Software as well as open standards (another related issue).

Conclusion

In this chapter we have outlined the main organizations involved in OSS. There are two groups, the FSF and OSI, who are primarily advocacy organizations. There are also several official bodies coordinating the largest and most well-known OSS projects. The commercial landscape of OSS is becoming crowded, with a number of pure-play and hybrid companies attempting to succeed in the OSS marketplace. Finally, there are major standards bodies like the W3C and IETF, and related movements like Open Content and Open Hardware, who feature prominently in the day-to-day life of the OSS community.

4

Deriving a framework
for analyzing OSS

In this chapter we derive a framework in which to analyze the OSS phenomenon. The framework is based on two influential models for understanding software systems and system development, namely Zachman's IS Architecture framework, and Checkland's CATWOE framework from Soft Systems Method (SSM). The categories of the resultant framework are used to discuss and elaborate the OSS phenomenon in a structured fashion.

Given the amount of descriptive detail already in print about OSS, the heterogeneity of the environments in which it is being pioneered, and the many meanings that have been ascribed to it (Gacek *et al.*, 2001), there is a need for some kind of organizing framework which could serve as a lens to facilitate an analysis of the OSS phenomenon. There are no universally accepted models for studying or evaluating software development. We have focused on two influential frameworks, namely Zachman's framework for information systems architecture (ISA) (Zachman, 1987; Sowa and Zachman, 1992), and the CATWOE framework from Checkland's Soft Systems Methodology (SSM) (Checkland, 1981; Checkland and Scholes, 1990; Checkland and Holwell, 1998). Each of these frameworks has particular strengths in complementary areas, and we have drawn upon both to derive a framework with which to analyze the OSS development phenomenon.

In this chapter, we begin by discussing both Zachman's ISA framework and Checkland's CATWOE framework, before articulating the derived framework that serves as our primary analytical tool for the remainder of the book. When one proposes any model or framework, it is useful to recall George Box's extremely apt observation that while "all models are wrong, some are useful" (Box, 1979). This framework, by necessity, simplifies certain aspects of the OSS approach. However, we believe it serves as a useful tool for highlighting certain significant issues in relation to OSS, and allowing a more rigorous and structured discussion of the phenomenon.

Zachman's framework for IS architecture

In what is recognized as a particularly influential contribution,[1] Zachman (1987; Sowa and Zachman, 1992) has drawn on the disciplines of architecture and structural engineering to derive a framework for IS architecture. In doing so, he was one of the first researchers to methodically explore the synergies between architecture and software engineering. This frame of reference has, of course, become increasingly popular. One notable example is in the area of object-oriented analysis and design, where the architectural theories of Christopher Alexander (Alexander *et al.*, 1977) have been heavily drawn upon (e.g. Gamma *et al.*, 1994).

Zachman's initial motivation for developing the ISA framework was the extraordinary growth he witnessed in the complexity of information systems, noting that in earlier eras (the 1950s, for example) the relative simplicity of systems did not require such a framework. We would argue that most Open Source Software projects compound a high level of technological complexity with the inherent complications of Internet-based distributed parallel development, and are thus in even greater need of such an analytical

---

[1] According to the *Web of Science Citation Database*, Zachman's ISA has been cited in over 70 scientific articles since its first publication (query performed at http://wos.heanet.ie/ on May 7, 2001).

framework. It should be noted, however, that Zachman's framework was created to better define (and thus control) the components within a system, not the development process itself, which means his ISA framework needs to be adapted to the task at hand. In some ways, however, Zachman anticipated this "port" of ISA, predicting in the 1987 paper that ISA will be valuable for "placing a wide variety of tools and/or methodologies in relation to one another." The framework has already been applied in this fashion by a number of researchers (e.g., Fitzgerald and Fitzgerald, 1999; Lyytinen *et al.*, 1998; Mercurio *et al.*, 1990; Montgomery, 1991).

Zachman's framework involves six descriptive categories, three of which are discussed in detail in the 1987 paper. While the remaining three are only briefly described in that paper, they are elaborated in depth in the 1992 paper. All six categories are summarized below.

- Material-oriented description – The first category focuses on the structure of the system, i.e., "what the thing is made of." In IS, such a description might take the form of an entity relationship diagram or similar data model.

- Function-oriented description – The second category focuses on the transformative aspects of the system, i.e., "how the thing works." In IS, such a description might take the form of a data flow diagram or similar process model.

- Location-oriented description – The third category focuses on the flows within the system, i.e., "where the connections exist." In IS, network models are an example of this kind of description.

- People-oriented description – The fourth category focuses on responsibility, i.e., "who is doing what." In the context of IS, examples might include organizational charts or user interface architectures.

- Time-oriented description – The fifth category focuses on the dynamics of the system over time, i.e., "when events take place." IS analogues include control structure charts or state transition diagrams.

■ Purpose-oriented description – The sixth and final category focuses on motivation, i.e., "why choices are made." Business strategy plans or knowledge definition charts would fall into this category.

CATWOE and Soft Systems Method

Early approaches to software development tended to consider development from a very technical or engineering perspective, manifesting itself in a stream of literature from the 1960s which focuses on the "software crisis" with expressions of concern about excessive expenditure and poor productivity in software development. As a consequence, the solutions that have been proposed have been essentially of a "hard" technical nature, e.g., proposing the adoption of more engineering-like development practices. This stream of literature has had a major effect on the teaching and practice of software development. However, another stream of literature, which began around the same time, was concerned with "soft" social issues such as user relations, the rise of technocracy, and consequences of computer system malfunction (see Friedman, 1989). This literature did not have the same immediate effect on software development practice as the first stream. However, in recent times the literature on software development and the literature on the implications of technology for users have been merging. This has led to a consideration of softer approaches to development.

The soft approaches to development have primarily been associated with Scandinavia (a notable exception being Checkland's Soft Systems Method (SSM) from the UK). It is worth noting, however, that there are significant cultural differences between Scandinavian and US society, a fact that some commentators have noted in discussing the significance of Linus Torvalds being Finnish. Floyd *et al.* (1989), in their outline of the background to Scandinavian approaches, refer to the emphasis in Scandinavian society on quality of life, worker participation, and the like. Other researchers in the area have also noted the differences between Scandinavian society and other societies. For example, Bjorn-Andersen (1988) reports an example of different advertising strategies for office automation in Scandinavia and the US. In the latter, the emphasis was on cost efficiency and ease of learning, which served to reduce training costs. However, for the same product in Scandinavia, the emphasis was on creating a better work environment, eliminating routine work, and creating more challenging jobs. Bjorn-Andersen links this difference, in part, to trade union influence in working practices, which seek to eliminate the dehumanizing and deskilling of work.

The Soft Systems Method is one that has been derived experientially based on the distillation of learning from a large number of "action research" projects. It is fully documented in Checkland (1981), with modifications and elaborations in Checkland and Scholes (1990), and Checkland and Holwell (1998). The method represents a paradigm shift for systems development in that most development methods are based upon the paradigm of optimization whereas SSM adopts a learning paradigm which recognizes "ill structured (soft) problems to which there are no such thing as 'right', or optimized, answers" (Wilson, 1984). Avison *et al.* (1992) clarify the difference between hard and soft systems thinking as follows:

> … in hard systems thinking a goal is assumed. The analyst modifies the system in some way so that a goal is achieved in the most efficient manner. The analysts identify a problem to be 'solved' and attempt to solve it. Hard systems thinking is concerned about the 'how' of the problem. In soft systems thinking, on the other hand, the objectives of the system are assumed to be more complex than a simple goal that can be achieved and measured. Understanding can be achieved through debate with all the 'actors' and emphasis is placed on the 'what' of the system. The analyst is not concerned with 'the' problem, but a situation in which problems exist—hence the term problem situation.

The SSM approach acknowledges the importance of people in an organizational context, and attempts to make sense of complex human activity systems, which are characterized by fuzzy or messy problem situations. SSM allows the problem situation to be studied from many points of view, thus ensuring a better understanding of the complexities of the situation. SSM also recognizes that the analyst cannot be neutral but is governed by an inherent *weltanschauung* – the world view encompassing the assumptions and mindset of the analyst. Ethical, political, and social issues have also been explicitly recognized and accorded a prominent role in SSM.

Checkland (1981) has proposed the CATWOE framework as an integral part of the SSM method. The term CATWOE itself is an acronym for Client, Actor, Transformation, *Weltanschauung*, Owner, and Environment, each of which is described below.

- *Clients* may be internal or external to the system, and represent the beneficiaries (or victims) affected by the system's activities.

- *Actors* are the agents within the system itself who carry out, or cause to be carried out, the main activities of the system.

- *Transformation* refers to the core of the system and the means by which inputs are transformed into defined outputs.

- *Weltanschauung* refers to the world-view or assumptions that underpin the process. It is recognized that there may be more than one *weltanschauung*, specific to the individual stakeholders involved.

- *Owner* refers to the agency that has prime concern for the system and the ultimate power in relation to whether the system continues to exist.

- *Environment* represents the wider systems of which the activity or system is a part, which must be taken as given, and which may impose certain constraints.

Deriving an analytical framework for OSS

Zachman's framework is essentially characteristic of the hard approach to software development. It is particularly comprehensive in its treatment of the function, data, and time aspects of development, which are generally accepted as the most important perspectives in the hard view of software development. It also considers network aspects explicitly in the "location" category. The network perspective is of increased importance in the context of modern software development as it is so much a feature of systems in the current Internet and web-enabled environment. This perspective is vital in the OSS approach, which is characterized by collaborative development among pan-globally distributed developers.

However, Zachman's framework is less comprehensive in relation to the "people" and "purpose" categories. These are vitally important categories in the OSS approach, since the stakeholders involved in OSS are many and varied. For example, it is not the case that all OSS developers are idealistic hackers contributing for free in their spare time. A study of the FreeBSD Project (to cite just one example) has revealed that 41 percent of developers were paid by their employers for their OSS work (Jorgensen, 2001). The CATWOE framework places a great deal of emphasis on the human and cultural aspects of systems development – aspects that do not feature prominently in most traditional software development methods, but which are a core element in OSS projects (Norin and Stöckel, 1998). Thus, the CATWOE framework significantly elaborates the "people" category in identifying the other stakeholder elements of *client*, *actor*, and *owner*. Similarly, the use of the extremely rich *weltanschauung* concept makes the CATWOE framework much more comprehensive in its treatment of the "purpose" category. The question "why?" is extremely important in understanding the OSS approach and the motivation underpinning the often *gratis* contributions of very talented developers.

Despite their different origins, it can be argued that there is quite a close correspondence between the Zachman and CATWOE framework elements. For example, in addition to the mapping from

Zachman's "people" category to the CATWOE *client, actor, owner* elements, the CATWOE *environment* element aligns with Zachman's "location" and "time" categories. Similarly, *transformation* and "function" can be paired, as can *weltanschauung* and "purpose." The synthesis of these two powerful frameworks provides a rich mechanism for a detailed analysis of the OSS approach. Thus, based on ISA and CATWOE, we have derived the following five categories for analyzing and describing Open Source Software as both a product and a process.

Qualification (what?)

Based primarily on Zachman's Material-Structural category, our Qualification category focuses on the question "What is Open Source Software?" This question is explored in Chapter 5 on two levels – first, what defines (qualifies) a system as being Open Source, and second, what material-structural characteristics (qualities) do these systems share?

Transformation (how?)

Our second category draws on Zachman's Function category and on Checkland's concept of Transformation. In Chapter 6, we explore how OSS inputs (the efforts of collaborative developers and the organizations and structures that support them) are transformed into OSS outputs (stable software releases). In other words, we ask "how is the OSS development process organized and realized?" as well as the related question "what tools are used (and how are they used) to support this process?"

Stakeholders (who?)

In this category, we rely upon Checkland to greatly enhance the expressibility of Zachman's People category. In Chapter 7, we analyze the various stakeholders in OSS – developers, users, companies, and organizations – in their various roles of clients, actors, and owners. In this context, we explore the characteristics of

- individual developers contributing to OSS projects;
- OSS software users;
- companies and not-for-profit organizations (NPOs) involved in OSS.

Environment (where and when?)

This category refers to both the geographic and temporal aspects of OSS development. In Chapter 8 we apply this category, looking at the online and offline spaces in which stakeholders interact, and the timing of events in OSS life cycles.

World-view (why?)

Finally, we use the motivation/*Weltanschauung* concepts to ask the question "Why OSS?" in Chapter 9. This question is posed on several levels. First, we investigate the technological world-view that supports participation in OSS. Next we examine the economic world-view in which OSS makes good career and business sense. Finally, we examine the socio-political world-view that underlies the motivation of many OSS participants. Each of these perspectives – technical, economic, and socio-political – are then further analyzed into the micro-level category of individual developers, and the macro-level category of communities.

Conclusion

In this chapter we have derived five analytical categories – qualification, transformation, stakeholders, environment, and world-view – through which to analyze the OSS phenomenon. We have coupled these with the set of simple interrogatives with which they equate – what, how, who, where, when, and why. This set of interrogatives was memorably captured by Rudyard Kipling, many years ago, and it is a debt we are happy to acknowledge:

> I keep six honest serving men
> (They taught me all I knew);
> Their names are What and Why and When
> And How and Where and Who
>
> POEM BY RUDYARD KIPLING, FOLLOWING ELEPHANT'S
> CHILD IN THE JUST SO STORIES.

Qualification: what defines a software system as Open Source?

Our first analytical category, Qualification, refers to both the identification (what products *qualify* as OSS?) and description (what *qualities* do OSS products share?) of Open Source Software products. This focus on products is unique to the Qualification category – the categories in the other chapters focus on OSS as a process. In this chapter, we

- articulate and justify a baseline definition of OSS products;

- categorize three large collections of OSS products, to determine the various levels of OSS presence in a variety of functional computing areas;

- describe some of the architectural and structural characteristics of OSS products.

Defining Open Source Software

We would argue that the most unambiguous and useful definition of OSS is the *Open Source Definition* as discussed in Chapter 1. In this section, we will demonstrate that this seemingly circular statement – that Open Source Software may be defined as software which fits the Open Source Definition – is in fact meaningful. The statement has two implications – necessity and sufficiency. First, the conformance of a software product's terms of distribution to all nine criteria of the OSD is *necessary* to qualify that product as a piece of Open Source Software. Second, conformance of a software product's terms of distribution to all nine criteria of the OSD, even without actual OSI certification, is *sufficient* for all intents and purposes.

OSD: nothing less will do

Most of the *popular* definitions of OSS – as represented by the many online technology dictionaries used as reference tools for mainstream managers and IT knowledge workers – characterize OSS based on only one or two OSD criteria. Frequently, OSS is defined simply as software with freely available source code (e.g., CMP, 2001; Computer User.com, 2001). These minimal definitions generally do not include commentary on either the significance, or the terms of use, associated with code availability. Even more thorough definitions (e.g., FOLDOC, 2001a), which explicitly define OSS as a method and philosophy for licensing and distributing software, fail to address the other aspects of the OSD. This leads to the perpetuation of decidedly false notions such as "Public Domain = Open Source" (see FOLDOC, 2001b).

The problem with such limited-criteria definitions is that, while they are accurately *inclusive* (yes, all OSS products have available source code), they are not accurately *exclusive* (not all products with available source code are OSS). By focusing on only one or two of the aspects evident in OSS products, the scope of the concept is extended to include decidedly "closed" software. Trial software, non-commercial use only software, and shareware, for example, are all available by free download and are redistributable, but do not provide available and modifiable source code, nor the freedom to use the software in any way the user sees fit. Likewise, proprietary but royalty-free libraries, which expose their source code, do so in a read-only manner (Feller and Fitzgerald, 2000). Using minimal definitions like those referenced above would qualify even *Microsoft* as an OSS developer! Microsoft (2001) has recently adopted an Open Source derivative called "Shared Source" which allows restricted access to source code to certain customers (some research institutions, top-tier independent software vendors (ISVs), leading original equipment manufacturers (OEMs), etc.). However, this model, which at a very superficial level may appear to be similar to OSS, differs fundamentally in that modification and redistribution are not permitted. Indeed, it may even be hazardous to the OSS movement in that viewing any of the Microsoft source might constitute grounds for a later claim for copyright violation if similar code appears in any OSS products.

Similarly, Hewlett-Packard is experimenting with an idea called "Corporate Source," which attempts to re-create OSS dynamics – but only within the internal HP community (Dinkelacker and Garg, 2001). In all of these examples, we see that defining a product as OSS, based on some but not all of the OSD criteria, leads to the inclusion of both unlicensed (public domain) and close-licensed (e.g., Internet Explorer, WinZip) software.

Stallman (1998) provides some examples of companies who have exploited the popularity of the concept and have created the impression of providing Open Source Software while not actually conforming to the required principles. At the extreme, he reports the case of Cygnus Solutions[1] who chose to advertise two *proprietary* products as follows:

> Cygnus Solutions is a leader in the Open Source market and has just launched two products into the Linux marketplace.

In this way, the company was able to exploit their other legitimate Open Source activity to create the impression that the software products under discussion were Open Source when in fact they were proprietary packages that did not come close to qualifying.

---

[1] Ironically, Cygnus Solutions, founded in 1989 before the Open Source term was coined or Linux was even developed, were probably the first commercial venture built on free software.

OSD: nothing more is needed

If nothing less than the whole nine yards (or, more to the point, whole nine criteria) will do, we must also demonstrate that nothing more is needed. Specifically, we call into question the definitive nature of the *OSI Certified* mark. More sophisticated definitions of OSS link the concept directly to the certification mark owned by the Open Source Initiative (e.g. Webopedia, 2001; Whatis?com, 2001; Raymond, 2001JFa). Raymond's definition, predictably, offers the most detail, explaining that the term was coined to

> be able to sell the hackers' ways of doing software to industry and the mainstream by avoiding the negative connotations (to suits) of the term "free software".[2]

The OSI serves an extremely important role within the OSS community and OSS industry. It acts as a standard builder, an advocacy campaigner, and a watchdog. As noted in Chapter 2, its existence and rhetoric stem from the authority of a 1998 summit attended by Eric Allman, Brian Behlendorf, Tim O'Reilly, Eric Raymond, Linus Torvalds, Guido van Rossum, Paul Vixie, Larry Wall, and Phil Zimmerman (O'Reilly.com, 1998), an admittedly small but certainly influential group. Its message has been widely received and adopted by the mass media and big business communities (Raymond, 2001RotH). A different specialist community – the academic researchers in computer science, information systems, software engineering, etc. – have likewise embraced the term "Open Source" and generally reference the conditions found in the OSD when discussing software like Linux, Apache, and Perl. However, we must be wary of the expressive power of definitions which state "OSS is software which has received the *OSI Certified* mark" but

---

[2] It's worth noting that elsewhere in the *Jargon File* we find "suit" defined as a "person who habitually wears suits, as distinct from a techie or hacker. See pointy-haired, burble, management, Stupids, SNAFU principle, PHB, and brain-damaged" (Raymond, 2001JFb).

which do not explicitly point to the Open Source Definition which underlies this certification.

While definitions hinged on one or two criteria are too inclusive to be useful, those dependent on a certification status are too *exclusive*. At the time of writing, there are only 21 licenses that have earned the OSI certification mark (Open Source Initiative, 2001a). While these 21 licenses cover thousands of products, it is naive to think that (a) all of these products actually bear the certification mark and (b) that there are not fully OSD-compliant licenses which simply do not appear on the list. It is true that all *OSI Certified* products are Open Source (i.e., distributed under terms compliant with the OSD), but not all OSD-compliant products are *OSI Certified*.

The problem is ultimately administrative. The OSI does not possess the resources or inclination to go out in a proactive manner and compare the licensing terms of every new and existing software product against the OSD. Rather, software developers who desire to use the mark must either (1) adopt, unchanged, a license already on the list (this is termed "self-certification"), or (2) invite the OSI to review a new license. As we discussed before, these developers may then use the *OSI Certified* mark, which is simply a notice stating either "This software is OSI Certified Open Source Software. OSI Certified is a certification mark of the Open Source Initiative." or "OSI Certified Open Source Software." (Open Source Initiative, 2001d). Because the burden is on the developer to initiate the process, it is perfectly possible for OSD-compliant software to live out its life without ever displaying the *OSI Certified* mark.

For example, Digital Creations' Zope is an extremely popular OSS web application server. However, the Zope Public License (ZPL) (Zope.org, 2001b), which is substantively identical to the Apache License, does not appear on the OSI list (Open Source Initiative, 2001a). Nor does Zope carry the *OSI Certified* statements; instead, the ZPL states, "This license has been certified as Open Source." (Zope.org, 2001b) and elsewhere "This license has received OSD branding. Digital Creations is working to stay true to the spirit of the Open Source Definition and its stated rationales." (Zope.org, 2001a). The fact that the ZPL is not on the list is an OSI administrative decision – since the ZPL is basically the Apache License, adding it to the list doesn't add value. More significant is the fact that Zope, who claim that they are fully certified,[3] apparently choose not to bear the actual *OSI Certified* mark. Zope represents a case-in-point that Open Source Software exists without the mark, and therefore OSI certification cannot be considered a defining feature.

The OSI certification process addresses the community's need for a trusted standards body that will consistently interpret both new licenses and the OSD criteria. However, while the *OSI Certified* mark is certainly a characteristic of many OSS products, we do not feel it can serve as the defining characteristic. It is only the OSD itself, no more, no less, which is both sufficiently inclusive and sufficiently exclusive to unambiguously define (based on its terms of distribution) a particular product as OSS/non-OSS.

There are two more definition-related questions remaining. First, we need to ask what role does the OSS development process (as discussed in the next few chapters) play in defining a product as Open Source? If Microsoft's Office 2000 suite is released under Larry Wall's *Artistic License*, does it instantly become Open Source? Or does the OSS identity of a product, in the community's eye, depend in part on the way in which it is actually developed and maintained?

Second, and perhaps more importantly, while the OSD is a solid rubric for defining a product as OSS, it is also somewhat imperialistic. There are a number of products using the Free Software Foundation's GPL which fully conform to the OSD. One could thus say that GPL-licensed software, like the GNU Emacs editor, is Open Source. But the creators of that software might disagree, insisting that GNU emacs, for example, is *Free Software*, not Open Source. Although Stallman (1998) notes that the "term 'Open Source' software is used by some people to mean more or less the same thing as free software," he nonetheless argues strongly

---

[3] Gary Graham, May 29, 2001, personal email.

that the latter is more accurate. This leaves us with the OSD as a useful tool for accurately answering the question "Is this software Open Source?" but with the lingering doubt, from one part of the development community, as to whether we are asking the wrong question.

Categorizing Open Source Software

In this section, we move from questions of definition to questions of categorization. We identify the broad trends that emerge in mapping representative groups of OSS products into major software categories. Specifically, we examine

- 333 applications projects (both active and pending) from Cosource, a commercial many-to-many auction site which matches independent developers to corporate (and private) clients (Cosource.com, 2001);

- 711 projects (at various stages of maturity) from Freshmeat, a not-for-profit OSS project directory (Freshmeat, 2001a);

- 580 stable software packages included in the official Red Hat Linux 6.0 distribution (Red Hat, 2001b).

Each of these sample groups has something to contribute to our understanding of OSS. The projects currently mediated by Cosource give us a broad picture of the functional areas that interest the commercial users of OSS products – mainly corporate IT shops who have adopted OSS products and need to maintain or extend these products. The projects indexed by Freshmeat give us insight into the needs and wants of the grassroots OSS community – to paraphrase Raymond (2001CatB) we see what "itches" are currently being scratched in the Bazaar. Finally, the official Red Hat release allows us to profile a stable and fully integrated suite of mature OSS products. The Red Hat release also allows us to determine in which software areas OSS users appear to enjoy the most freedom of choice.

Cosource

Briefly stated, Cosource solicits requests from individuals and companies who require new OSS products, or improvements to existing products, and match them both with developers who are willing to build the software and with other individuals and companies who are willing to share the cost. At the time of writing, Cosource listed 333 active and pending projects under the umbrella term, Applications. Figure 5.1 shows the number of projects by category within the Applications group (the category labels are those used by Cosource).

The most active functional categories are *Internet* (around 19 percent of total) and *Drivers* (around 16 percent of total). The *Internet* category is divided evenly between

- client applications – "Web Application Testing Utility" and "BeOS Port of Speak Freely Internet Telephony App," and

- server applications – "stabilize and improve telechat 1.0."

In the *Drivers* category,

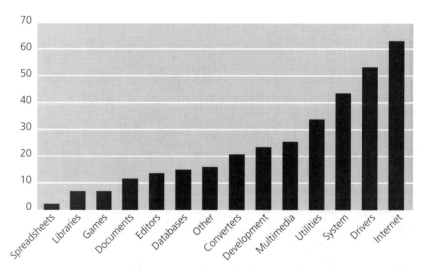

FIGURE 5.1 Categories of software projects in the Cosource Applications group

- network drivers – "ISDN support for BeOS" and "Bluetooth protocol stack for Linux,"

- audio drivers – "BeOS driver for Digigram VX Pocket soundcard," and

- miscellaneous drivers – "Casio BX-20 PC-UNITE synch tool for UNIX"

account for nearly 75 percent of the category. The remaining 25 percent deal with graphics, printers, and databases.

The next most active categories are *System* (around 12 percent of total) and *Utilities* (around 10 percent of total). The *System* category includes emulation, kernel, file, and graphics-oriented projects such as "Snapshot of Filesystem for Backups," "Directory quota for Linux," and "Finish ssh proxy." The *Utilities* category contains projects like "Open Source OCR software." Lagging just behind *System* and *Utilities* are the somewhat active categories of *Converters* ("LaTeX/TeX to a format MS Word can understand"), *Development* ("Simple Project Management App for BeOS"), and *Multimedia* ("Add AVI support to Wine"). The remaining categories (*Spreadsheets*, *Libraries*, *Games*, *Documents*, *Editors*, *Databases*, and *Other*) have comparatively little activity.

Based on this snapshot of activity at Cosource, we can identify two key trends. First, we see evidence that the Cosource client community is primarily interested in OSS products that support the exploitation of Internet and other network technologies. Second, we see a broad disparity between demand for low-level drivers and utilities on the one hand, and end-user applications on the other. It is also worth noting that there is demonstrated interest in BeOS, which runs a close second to Linux in terms of activity. Together the two platforms make up 58 percent of Cosource's 159 platform-specific project requests.

Freshmeat

Like Cosource, we discussed Freshmeat in Chapter 3. Freshmeat is the largest web index of independent Open Source software projects and a part of the Open Source Development Network. At the time of writing, Freshmeat had indexed 711 Open Source projects, divided into 17 top-level categories. Figure 5.2 shows the number of projects within each category. The category labels are those used by Freshmeat, with the exception of the *Religion* category (3 projects), which we combined with the 28 projects in *Other*.

As with Cosource, the most active Freshmeat category is *Internet*, which accounts for 14 percent of the total number of projects. The *Internet* category contains a variety of applications, for the most part related to File Transfer Protocol (FTP), log analysis, the Domain Name Service (DNS), and Hypertext Transfer Protocol (HTTP). Unlike Cosource, the next two most active categories are *Software Development* and *Games/Entertainment*. The *Software Development* category contains a number of build tools, code generators, compilers/interpreters, debuggers, and libraries. Notably, the least active areas in this category were quality assurance, testing, and version control tools. The *Games/Entertainment* category contained both games (e.g., Armagetron and Q3Master) and game development tools (e.g., the pygame libraries).

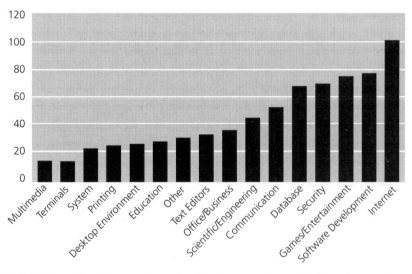

FIGURE 5.2 Categories of software projects in Freshmeat's top-level index

Lest we convey the impression that the main itch among independent OSS developers is a Quake-induced itchy-trigger finger, it's worth noting that *Database* (a category woefully under-represented at Cosource) and *Security* are both only a few projects shy of overtaking the *Games/Entertainment* category. The Freshmeat *Database* category includes servers like PostgreSQL, front ends like Gedafe (Generic Database Front-End), data modeling tools like Alzabo (Perl-based RDBMS-OO mapping), and many, many web-database integration tools and platforms. The *Security* category includes software like fwlogwatch (firewall log analyzer), Guarddog (firewall management utility), and ssh-multiadd (ssh keys management utility).

Two more categories, *Scientific/Engineering* and *Communication*, demonstrated a fairly high level of developer activity. *Scientific/ Engineering* applications tend to be low-level research tools, like Gnome Flow (calculate and visualize simple steady-state fluid flows) and RandomCsp (generate binary constraint satisfaction test problems). The *Communication* applications include news and mail servers and clients, as well as synchronous tools like SILC (Secure Internet Live Conferencing). The remaining categories – *Multimedia* (mostly audio), *Terminals* (mostly emulators), *System* (mostly administration), *Printing* (drivers and converters), *Desktop Environment* (almost all GNOME and KDE), *Education* (typing tutors, etc.), *Text Editors*, *Office/Business*, and *Other* – had comparatively less activity.

Although this is a cursory analysis of the Freshmeat development domain, we do see some interesting trends. It's worth noting, though not surprising, that the business community represented by Cosource and the grassroots community indexed by Freshmeat share a dominant interest in Internet-related software development. It is also significant that the most active areas of development at Cosource dealt with device drivers and systems functionality, while the Freshmeat community demonstrated greater interest in development tools and games – the work and play of the wider OSS community. The levels of activity at Freshmeat likewise point to the academic/scientific roots of Open Source and Free Software, with sustained activity in the areas of scientific tools and database systems. Finally, it is interesting to note that although there are many projects building development tools, there are very few analysis and design tools available, a gap in the OSS tool kit noted by Bittman *et al.* (2001).

Red Hat Linux 6.0

Red Hat is perhaps the largest (500+ employees) and most widely recognized OSS company, and is the leader in Linux distribution to the corporate market. There are two benefits to be gained from examining the software packages included in an official Red Hat distribution (in this case, 6.0). First, a Red Hat distribution represents a collection of well-tested, stable applications; the Cosource and Freshmeat sample areas include software in various states of development. Second, very few users install all of the packages that come with a Red Hat distribution, as there is considerable redundancy within software categories. Thus, analyzing such a distribution gives us a sense of where OSS users may enjoy the most choice. Figure 5.3 shows the

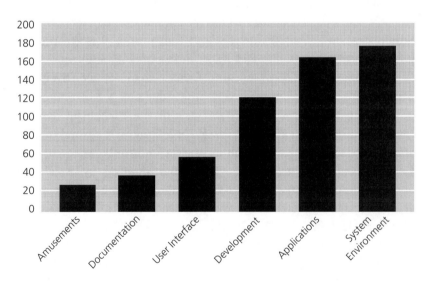

FIGURE 5.3 Categories of software packages in Red Hat Linux 6.0

number of packages in each of six categories. The category labels are those used by Red Hat.

The largest collection of packages in the distribution falls into the *System Environment* category. Although *System Environment* is the largest category, there is not a great deal of choice involved in the installation process; almost all of the packages are required for a functional system. *System Environment* includes the actual Linux kernel (vmlinuz), basic system environment software (like LILO, which boots the system), daemons (system and server processes like DHCP, Squid (proxy caching), and the optional Apache HTTP server), libraries (like XFree86-libs and gnome-libs), and command-line shells like Bash (the Bourne Again SHell).

The next largest category in the distribution is *Applications*. This category is divided into 13 areas. The largest area is System, which contains packages associated with system-level operations. Examples include Comanche (COnfiguration MANager for apaCHE) and gnome-linuxconf (system configuration). Running a close second is a collection of Internet applications like Fetchmail, ncftp, and Netscape Communicator. The next largest group is Multimedia, with software like GIMP (GNU Image Manipulation Program) and mpg123 (MPG player), followed by Publishing applications like Ghostscript, xpdf, and TeTeX. The distribution also comes with a number of communications applications (tools for dial-up, login, fax, etc.), nearly 20 text editors (like emacs, joe, and vim), and a dozen text manipulation tools like gawk (the GNU version of awk). There is also a decent collection of archiving packages (like tar and gzip). The smallest *Applications* package areas deal with file management, productivity, engineering, emulators, and databases (only postgresql is included).

Red Hat has gathered all development tools into a separate category, which is nearly as large as the combined *Applications* category discussed above. The *Development* category includes debuggers, languages (C/C++, Perl, Python, TCL, and Scheme, among others), libraries, tools associated with building system-level software, and general development tools like automake and autoconf. The *User Interface* category contains packages associated with various desktop environments and the X Window System. The *Documentation* category is deceptively large, as it contains multiple translations of the same documents, and includes documentation for the Red Hat system as a whole, and for specific packages like GIMP and sendmail. The smallest category, *Amusements*, is fairly evenly divided between games (of the Tetris and Solitaire variety) and entertaining graphics (screensavers, Mandelbrot set generators, etc.)

It is not really surprising that the largest collection of software in the distribution – both in its own category and as part of the *Applications* category – deals with basic Operating System functionality. This is, after all, an Operating System distribution. By pushing this collection of system software to the side, we get a picture of the kinds of software available for running on top of the Red Hat Linux platform. First, we see a predominance of Internet and development-related applications, reflecting the trends noted in the Freshmeat index. Again, the suite of development tools is focused on the implementation aspects of software development – there is a conspicuous lack of tools for analysis and design. Second, we see much more choice in the area of production (multimedia, publishing, editing) than in the area of productivity (end-user business tools).[4] Finally, we see a dramatic lack of choice in the database software,[5] which might serve to explain the interest evident in the topic at Freshmeat.

Specific characteristics of Open Source Software

Having developed a composite picture of the categorical trends found in representative collections of Open Source Software, we

---

[4] As mentioned previously, there are several office suites in the making, such as GNOME Office and OpenOffice.

[5] There are, of course, Open Source databases in the market. MySQL has proved extremely popular as a tool for building web-database applications, and PostgreSQL is at the heart of the new Red Hat Database.

turn now to the more specific characteristics of OSS applications. In particular, we look at

- the programming languages and paradigms favored by the OSS development community;

- the strong modularity characteristic of OSS products; and

- the relative complexity of OSS products.

Programming languages

Based on another view of the Freshmeat directory (2001b), we get a picture of the main programming languages, and thus programming paradigms, employed by the OSS community.

The most common programming language – used in almost a third of the projects listed – was C. This probably reflects the fact that C has become the language of choice for low-level systems programming; in the past, assembler would have been use for such programming.

Object-oriented (OO) languages like Ada, C++, Dylan, Eiffel, Java, Objective C, Ruby, Smalltalk, etc., were used in a quarter of the projects. The most common OO language was C++, reinforcing the OSS affinity for the C language. A strong trend towards OO programming is not too surprising, as object-orientation supports modular development and component-based reuse, common aspects of OSS products (see below) and the OSS development process (see Chapter 6).

Another quarter of the projects listed were written using the full-featured scripting languages Perl, Python, and Tcl. It should be noted that OSD-compliant interpreters for all three of these languages are available, thus they provide an example of the Open Source community's habit of bootstrapping – using OSS products to build more OSS products. A similar phenomenon occurs with the OSS configuration management product, CVS, which, although inferior to some proprietary alternatives, is very widely used in the OSS community (CVS is discussed in more detail in Chapter 6).

Another common development platform is PHP, a hypertext-pre-processing Apache module.

Fewer projects used query languages (SQL and PL/SQL), functional languages (Haskell and ML), recursive languages (Lisp and Scheme), or assembly language. *Very* few projects used Fortran, Pascal, or 4GLs (Visual Basic or Delphi). No projects used APL, ASP, Cold Fusion, Erlang, Euler, Euphoria, Logo, Object Pascal, PROGRESS, Prolog, Simula, or Xbasic (although they were listed on the Freshmeat site). This suggests that despite some claims, the involvement of the non-technically literate as code contributors is not a feature of OSS, as they might be reasonably expected to use these high-productivity tools.

One of the most often identified characteristics of OSS is its tendency towards modularity. The architecture of the Apache Web Server, for example, is completely modular. The actual Apache distribution includes around 40 separate modules (see Table 5.1), each handling different aspects of Apache functionality, and each capable of independent modification and evolution.

TABLE 5.1 Apache modules

Module	Function
Core	Core Apache features
threaded	Threading via Pthreads
mpm_winnt	Multi-processing module
perchild	Multi-processing module
prefork	Non-threaded processes model
mod_access	Access control
mod_actions	Executing CGI scripts
mod_alias	Mapping host file systems
mod_asis	HTTP headers
mod_auth	User authentication
mod_auth_anon	Anonymous user access
mod_auth_db	User authentication
mod_auth_dbm	User authentication

FIGURE 5.1 continued

Module	Function
mod_auth_digest	MD5 authentication
mod_autoindex	Automatic directory listings
mod_cern_meta	Support for HTTP header metafiles
mod_cgi	Invoking CGI scripts
mod_cgid	Invoking CGI scripts
mod_charset_lite	Character set translation
mod_dav	WebDAV HTTP extensions
mod_dir	Basic directory handling
mod_env	Passing of environments to CGI scripts
mod_example	Demonstrates Apache API
mod_expires	Apply expires: headers to resources
mod_ext_filter	Filtering output with external programs
mod_file_cache	Caching files in memory for faster serving
mod_headers	Add arbitrary HTTP headers to resources
mod_imap	The imagemap file handler
mod_include	Server-parsed documents
mod_info	Server configuration information
mod_isapi	Windows ISAPI Extension support
mod_log_config	User-configurable logging
mod_mime	Determining document types
mod_mime_magic	Determining document types
mod_negotiation	Content negotiation
mod_proxy	Caching proxy abilities
mod_rewrite	URI-to-filename mapping
mod_setenvif	Environment variables
mod_so	Support for loading modules at runtime
mod_speling	Automatically correct minor typos in URLs
mod_status	Server status display
mod_unique_id	Generate unique request identifiers
mod_userdir	User home directories
mod_usertrack	User tracking using cookies
mod_vhost_alias	Dynamically configured mass virtual hosting

(Modified from Apache Software Foundation, 2001a)

In addition to the modules included in the standard distribution, there are an enormous number of Perl modules, which extend the functionality of the Apache Web Server. These modules cover a variety of functional areas, including Active Server Pages, Java Server Pages, BBS systems, file compression, embedded Perl, documentation systems, dynamic navigation, FTP, NNTP, SSI, security systems, LDAP, NIS, database integration, XML, caching, integration with Apache C structures and modules, HTTP method handlers, watchdog and monitoring tools, development and debugging tools, etc. (MacEachern, 2001).

Like Apache, the well-known OSS language, Perl, has elevated the modularity concept to new extremes. At the time of writing, there are well over 1,000 Perl modules centrally located at CPAN.[6] Modules are not standalone scripts – they are reusable software components and support the highly collaborative, parallel development process described in Chapter 6. Perl modules are independently developed packages that provide a class of the same name as the module, and import and output methods that allow the module to be used in a fairly transparent fashion. The following are a snapshot of a few areas for which Perl modules have been developed:

- operating system interfaces;

- hardware drivers, networking, device control, and inter-process communication;

- data types and database interfaces;

- user interfaces;

- emulations of other programming languages;

- option, argument, parameter, and configuration file processing;

- internationalization;

- authentication, security, and encryption;

---

[6] http://www.perl.com/CPAN-local/modules/

- World Wide Web, HTML, HTTP, CGI, Internet Mail, Usenet News, MIME, etc.;

- archiving, compression, and conversion;

- interface modules to commercial software.

Complexity

Finally, a brief characterization of the complexity of OSS products is relevant. On the one hand, large OSS products (like the Linux kernel, the Mozilla browser, and the VIM text editor), as a result of modular architectures and decentralized parallel development, are quite complex (Godfrey and Lee, 2000; Godfrey and Tu, 2000; Tran *et al.*, 2000). On the other hand, the bulk of OSS applications (system utilities, compilers and interpreters, device drivers, implementations of networking protocols, etc.) belong to software engineering domains where the general requirements and the architectural reference models are well known and accepted, even if complex (Aoki *et al.*, 2001; Shaw and Garlan, 1996). Michael Kay (2001), developer of Saxon (an XML Stylesheet Language Transformation processor), writes:

> Another important consideration is that the specification and requirements are clear. I don't think I could have written Saxon and designed the XSLT language at the same time. Writing to a specification produced by someone else is an important discipline: It prevents succumbing to the developer's temptation to make the specification fit the code rather than the other way round, and it reduces the time spent chasing up cul-de-sacs.

Likewise, Bezroukov (1999b) introduces the notion of "having a tail-light to follow" as a fundamental organizing principle in OSS. Many OSS projects are implementations of complex but well-understood specifications. The apparent complexity serves as an attraction as it represents a challenge for the OSS programmer. The well-understood requirements facilitate the distributed, parallel process that characterizes OSS (see Chapter 6).

Scacchi (2001) has carried out a detailed study of how requirements are specified and understood across a diverse range of OSS communities. It is especially striking in one community, who work on X-ray astronomy and deep space imaging, that developers require deep knowledge of the application domain to be able to make sense of the requirements in the first place, and the lessons and techniques of conventional requirements analysis are of little benefit.

Conclusion

In this chapter we have addressed the qualification of Open Source Software. First, we identified the OSD as the most useful definition for identifying OSS products, and noted that a number of types of closed software conform to some, but not all, of the OSD criteria. We have further argued that OSI certification, while useful, cannot be considered an essential part of the definition.

In our exercise in categorization, we have seen that there is a dominant interest in Internet systems, which makes perfect sense since the Internet is the enabling environment of the OSS development process. We have also seen that while the corporate user community demonstrates an interest in extending system functionality and hardware support, the wider development community is primarily interested in development tools, entertainment, and research software.

Other characteristics are evident as well. We see a predilection within the community towards low-level programming languages (C), followed by object-orientation and Open Source interpreted languages. We likewise see in major OSS products, a high level of modularity, coupled with complex, but widely understood and accepted architectural reference models. At the same time, we get the sense that many OSS products do not tend to be conceptually complex; rather, they tend to be in well-defined software engineering domains. However, in specific domains which are highly complex, the deep domain knowledge of the individual developers ensures that requirements are understood.

6

Transformation: how is the Open Source process organized and managed?

In this chapter we address the Transformation category of our framework, asking the question "How does OSS development take place?" We describe the most common methods and tools used in OSS development, examine the norms and taboos that govern OSS in the absence of conventional project management, and discuss the OSS development life cycle.

The OSS development process

As previously discussed, the decades-old notion of the software crisis asserts that software suffers from taking too long and costing too much to develop, and not working very well when it's eventually delivered. While some have argued that the software crisis is an exaggeration, and that software is the success story of our time (Glass, 1998), it has also been argued that there will never be a "silver bullet" to solve the software crisis and that radical improvement in software development is unlikely ever to occur (Brooks, 1987). However, such a claim is reminiscent of the famous reported declaration in 1899 of Charles H. Duell, the US Commissioner of Patents, that "everything that can be invented has been invented."

According to many of its proponents, Open Source Software, or rather the OSS process, does in fact offer such a silver bullet,

The story goes that Duell resigned his position as Commissioner of Patents on the grounds of the above declaration. Unfortunately, spoiling a good story, it appears that such a declaration and subsequent resignation never happened. However, the IT field has many other examples of famously incorrect predictions, including those of Thomas Watson, IBM's chairman, who predicted that the total worldwide demand for computers would not exceed *five*, and, more recently, Ken Olson, President of DEC, who expressed the opinion that no one would ever need a computer at home, or Bill Gates's assertion that 640K of memory should be enough for everyone.

providing very reliable and high quality software both quickly and inexpensively (Jorgensen, 2001; Neumann, 2000a, 2000b; Raymond, 2001CatB), a point even grudgingly conceded by Microsoft in the infamous Halloween Documents (1998). As the OSI puts it: "mature open-source code is as bullet-proof as software ever gets" (Open Source Initiative, 2001e).

However, it should be noted at the outset that there is no "orthodox" OSS process – different developers and organizations employ different methods and tools. However, we are able to identify several characteristics that are common to most OSS projects. The generic OSS development process

■ is parallel, rather than linear;

■ involves large communities of globally distributed developers;

■ utilizes truly independent peer review;

■ provides prompt feedback to user and developer contributions;

■ includes the participation of highly talented, highly motivated developers;

■ includes increased levels of user involvement;

■ makes use of extremely rapid release schedules.

Below, we explore each of these characteristics in an effort to elaborate on the generic OSS development process. As we do so, certain other issues, such as the norms and taboos that govern development in the absence of conventional project management, and the use of tools in OSS, come into focus.

Parallel development

Parallel, rather than linear, development is a key characteristic of the OSS process, and is enabled by (and also perpetuates) the highly modular nature of many OSS products (see Chapter 5). Parallel development refers to the practice of individual (or small groups of) developers working on one aspect of a large system at the same time that other individuals (or groups) work on another aspect of the same system. As with parallel processing, i.e., breaking an application's instructions into discrete chunks that can be run in parallel rather than in sequence, parallel development can lead to tremendous performance gains. Specifically, parallel development makes it possible for a very large number of developers to collaborate efficiently – since they are working simultaneously rather than waiting on each other.

In a classic treatise on the software development process, Brooks (1995)[1] coined the widely accepted law that "adding manpower to a late software product makes it later." Brooks cited empirical evidence to support this from the development of the IBM 360 operating system. Thus, merely increasing the number of developers should not be a benefit in software development. However, under the OSS model, it would appear that Brooks' Law is side-stepped,[2] perhaps due to the fact that the various members of OSS projects do not *all* need to know *everything* about the project (communication costs are at the root of Brooks' Law), but rather work on *highly cohesive* tasks within *loosely coupled* groups.[3] Parallel development thus provides OSS projects with a net gain in terms of development speed.

Above, we said that parallel development involved *Developer A* working on one aspect of the system while *Developer B* worked on another aspect of the same system. This is not always the case, and

---

[1] Originally published in 1975.

[2] Which is not to say that the IBM 360 could have been developed using the OSS process.

[3] The terms cohesion and coupling are drawn from software engineering parlance, and in this context, refer to the fact that highly cohesive tasks have a single well-defined purpose, and that loosely coupled groups are ones that do not depend on other groups to perform the task at hand.

often *Developers A* and *B* are both working on the same component, but completely independently. The conventional wisdom of software engineering would suggest that this aspect of parallel development – redundancy – is potentially hazardous. Certainly, very few traditional software development projects would knowingly allow (let alone encourage) different sub-groups to work independently on the same task. Effective project management would in fact strive to ensure that the duplication (seen as a waste) of effort never occurs. Interestingly, the hacker ethic that underlies OSS development would seem to share this view. The three great virtues of programming have been identified as laziness, impatience, and hubris – the first two directly related to not reinventing the wheel (Wall, 1999). Likewise, Raymond has postulated, "Good programmers know what to write. Great ones know what to rewrite (and reuse)" (Raymond, 2001CatB). Despite this aversion to wasted effort found in both traditional and hacker development communities, most OSS projects strongly encourage exactly this kind of parallelism. Why? The main reason seems to be that the performance loss associated with redundancy is far outweighed by the quality gained from allowing multiple solutions to the same problem to compete with each other – in a process akin to natural selection. The fact that OSS projects have the luxury to work in this way is related to the size of the development community (see next section). Clearly, such a method is not feasible in most traditional development projects, but when the size of the development community numbers in the thousands, perhaps it is.

Thus, in situations where developers work on *different* components in parallel, development speed is improved. Conversely, in situations where developers work on *the same* components in parallel, product quality is improved.

Large, globally distributed development communities

As noted previously, the development communities involved in OSS projects are potentially both very large and international, even global in scope. The Apache HTTP Project, for example, has core developers from Canada, Germany, Italy, the US, and the UK (Fielding, 1999), and studies of the Linux kernel development community show activity in at least 28 countries (Hermann *et al.*, 2000). Likewise, an analysis of the developers of general Linux applications (Dempsey *et al.*, 1999) revealed tremendous activity in the US, Germany, the UK, Holland, Australia, France, Italy, Canada, Sweden, Finland, Austria, and the Czech Republic. This widely distributed community interacts and collaborates primarily using a wide variety of Internet technologies, as discussed later in this chapter and in Chapter 8. Asundi (2001) discusses the high level of communication among OSS developers, stating that some OSS projects run chat sites once a week to discuss development issues.

The global, or near global, nature of OSS communities improves the overall quality of OSS – both the process and its products – in many ways. For example, it means that functional requirements of Open Source software are, from the outset, determined from an international standpoint. Proprietary software is often developed primarily from a US-centric perspective, and localized after the fact. Raymond (2001CatB) describes how in the evolution of Fetchmail, he added some functionality that was relevant in an international context but not in the US. Thus, he was not aware of the requirement initially, but by building it in, the software had greater potential worldwide appeal.

The global nature of the OSS community also represents to many a dilution of the US influence in the software arena. As already mentioned, the Chinese government is interested in OSS for this reason. Also, Linus Torvalds being a Finn whose parents belonged to the Communist party has been portrayed as a significant advantage in some quarters (Leonard, 2000), despite the fact that Richard Stallman has had to fight hard to shed the same label (Stallman, 1992). Certainly, in terms of stimulating the contributions from students, who are in the (generally transitory) anarchistic and rebellious stage of their development, the underground, anti-establishment demeanor of OSS is highly attractive.

Truly independent peer review

Another advantage of a large, distributed development pool is that peer review, a mainstay of conventional software engineering, is truly independent. In a traditional development setting, peer review may be stymied somewhat by the fact that all the developers belong to the same organization and, even with the best will in the world, may not be motivated to dig deep and find errors. Of course, on the other hand, given the intense political and competitive nature of the workplace, it may be more likely that peers will strive very hard to condemn the work of colleagues, by artificially exaggerating any negative aspects. Either way, peer review is not guaranteed to be truly independent in traditional development environments.

In OSS, however, developers may never have met each other face-to-face, and will not have any reason to artificially confound the peer review process. Thus, the feedback is likely to be genuine. Also, because the communication is not face-to-face but via Internet mail, the tolerance for posturing and "noise" is lower. Indeed, the fact that the peer reviewers are not all known to the original developer, and may even include the universally respected "giants" of the field, probably serves as a huge motivator to submit for review only very high quality code in the first place.

Furthermore, peer review is taken to a new level in the OSS model – a kind of double-loop level of peer review. Firstly, code is submitted to the general OSS community for review and feedback, and then the suggestions and contributions from the community are reviewed again by the original author and the community, thus creating a cycle of peer review.

The OSS recipe of "shared knowledge + peer review" has struck many as being resonant of the academic model (cf. Bezroukov, 1999a, 1999b; Himanen, 2001). It has even prompted Andrew Leonard (2000) to argue half seriously that the Free Software/OSS movement began at

> ... the close of the 11th century, [when] an Italian jurist named Irnerius founded a school of law in the town of Bologna. We are told by

Odofredus, a 13th century professor of Roman law, that Irnerius was the first "to pass on his research through his teaching." This assertion may be questionable – no doubt there have been countless other scholars who taught what they had learned, long before Irnerius. (Aristotle and Confucius, to pick just two, spring to mind.) But the contention is intriguing. A central tenet of open-source faith is the belief that source code is an intellectual good that should be shared with as wide an audience as possible …

Prompt feedback

Peer review is powerful, and leads to what Raymond (2001CatB) has famously called Linus's Law of "Given enough eyeballs, all bugs are shallow." However, Linus's Law largely depends on the ability of the community to rapidly communicate bug reports, functionality requirements, etc. The OSS community uses a variety of Internet tools (discussed in detail in Chapter 8) to ensure that user-to-user, user-to-developer, and developer-to-developer communication is efficient. These tools are backed up with an ethos which

- recognizes quality contributions from any source – an important motivator for developers, and

- treats users as co-developers.

Feedback in OSS is rapid, and even continuous, since developers can work asynchronously in different time zones. Jorgensen (2001) describes it as a constant cycle of "see bug, fix bug, see bug fixed in new release" – dramatically different from the proprietary model of vendor-driven improvement schedules. There are many high-profile examples of the promptness of feedback in the OSS literature. For example, when Mozilla became Open Source, a group of developers from Australia contributed some encryption routines within hours. Likewise, the Ping of Death virus attack was resolved in the Linux world within hours. Schmidt and Porter (2001) also report on the promptness of the feedback loop in OSS:

Often it's only a matter of minutes or hours from the time a bug is reported from the periphery to the point at which an official patch is supplied from the core to fix it.

The issue of feedback in OSS is a vitally important one, and several authors have identified the fact that the vast majority of questions posed by OSS developers go unanswered (Ari, 2001; Ghosh and Prakash, 2000; McKusick, 1999; Mockus *et al.*, 2000), an issue that is discussed in more detail in Chapter 10. Yet, as already mentioned, the tolerance for noise must by necessity be low in OSS. Thus, the questions that are answered can stimulate a new level of awareness and learning within the community in general, as developers can learn the intricacies of the domain. This contributes towards the kind of community knowledge building that supplements the requirements specification process in OSS, as discussed by Scacchi (2001).

Highly talented, highly motivated developers

Many point to the high levels of ability and commitment demonstrated by OSS developers. We discuss motivation in detail in Chapter 9. Here, we focus on the issue of talent.

Attracting appropriately skilled software developers is a worldwide problem, and several studies have revealed the radically different levels of developer productivity in the software profession (Boehm, 1981; Brooks, 1987; Vitalari and Dickson, 1983). Indeed, it is now accepted that some developers (as many as one in five) are actually negative producers, i.e., they slow the others down. In OSS projects, of course, we find novice developers as well, but their participation does not necessarily slow down the overall pace of the project, since their contributions are made generally in areas appropriate to their skill level (Mockus *et al.*, 2000). While claims that OSS developers are drawn from the top 5 percent of the overall software development community (Raymond, 2001) are impossible to prove, it is certainly the case that the leading pioneers in the various OSS projects are in the very upper echelon of the programming profession (Cook, 2001).

The high level of skill evidenced by the core developers of many

OSS projects is critical to the success of these projects. First of all, core developer groups bring a far more sophisticated understanding of software engineering and architecture to bear on the project than the average contributor solving a specific localized problem. There are several examples (Linux and Sendmail, to name just two) that have demonstrated the importance of solid design and architecture for encouraging the growth and evolution of a project.

Also, the very reputation of highly skilled core developers often attracts other developers who are keen to work with these experts and to have their work vetted (and accepted) by them. Developers like Brian Behlendorf, Larry Wall, Alan Cox (the list goes on) have all earned enough respect in the community to act as arbiters – selecting certain contributions and rejecting others. In a reputation-driven culture, the supreme authority of a universally recognized gifted software leader, or acknowledged board of directors, is vital to prevent squabbles over "the right" to have one's code included. Given that conventional project management control is not possible, some unquestionable authority is ultimately necessary. The precise arrangements for vesting this authority vary in different OSS projects. MacLachlan (1999) reports on the issue: in the case of the Linux kernel, Torvalds has final say and is the supreme authority. By contrast, in the Apache Project, a group of about 20 core group members oversee changes, and any individual member of this core group has a right to veto. Somewhere in between is Perl whose governance is described by chief maintainer Chip Salzenberg as a "constitutional monarchy." While the creator of Perl, Larry Wall, has the ultimate say, day-to-day design decisions are made by Salzenberg (and other members of the Perl Porters group).

As might be expected, the authority of the lead developer or core group is not always appreciated. MacLachlan (1999) discusses the dictatorships that are evident in several OSS projects, although it has been suggested that the dictatorships are actually benevolent (Cook, 2001). Nonetheless, Moody (1997, cited in Bezroukov, 1999a) reports some interesting examples of dissension in the ranks of the OSS community, largely centering around ego-disputes, and typified by the following example from a BSD vs. Linux flame war:

It will be a cold day at the equator before L. Torvalds sets aside his ego for the sake of someone else's better ideas

Over time, of course, other talented developers prove themselves and take over various subsystems. They have been socialized into the ethos of the project, and understand the intricacies of the design and so on. Thus, the collaboration continues very efficiently, and the distribution of development is seamlessly and painlessly achieved.

The question arises: "Why do the most highly talented developers in the software profession (if this actually is the case) contribute their skills for free to OSS projects?" Given that skill shortages in software development is probably the most often cited problem in the industry, it would seem that money quite literally cannot buy these development skills, and yet they are often contributed freely under the OSS model. We return to this issue again in Chapter 9 where the motivations underpinning OSS are investigated.

Actively involved users

As many have pointed out, OSS is not just about highly talented code-gods. Users (read "people," not customers) also play an important role in OSS development – far more than in the proprietary software environment. They can, for example, elaborate requirements, test the functionality of what is being produced, and write documentation, all vital roles in development, but ones which programmers are traditionally reluctant to fulfill. Developer–user collaboration is at the heart of OSS, and Raymond (2001CatB) has argued that if developers treat their users as their most valuable resource, that is in fact what they become. OSS seems, at least partially, to invert the hierarchical order of coders, testers, and documenters seen in traditional software development environments. Also, as OSS influence begins to spread, there is evidence of models where users perform the majority of the testing task (Schmidt and Porter, 2001), or request new features (Aoki *et al.*, 2001).

Finally, we see evidence of tolerance for users not entirely technically competent in community websites like Linuxnewbie.org, where users can learn more about Linux and how to contribute.

There is less tolerance for novice activity in OSS products themselves. For example, when logging into a Linux system as `root`, the GNOME file manager provides the cheerful message that "as root, you can damage your system, and the File Manager will not stop you."

Rapid release schedule

In OSS, the size of the development pool, the promptness of communication and feedback, and the distribution of the essential development tasks all support a rapid incremental release pattern (Jorgensen, 2001). Raymond (2001CatB), for example, reports that new versions of the Linux kernel were being released at the rate of more than one per day at one stage in 1991. The OSS development process is focused on the product and the user of the product, and time-to-market is considered critical.

Tool support for OSS

There is more to the OSS process than a handful of best practice methods, and some discussion of the OSS toolkit is needed to complete the picture.

Given the global location of developers who seldom meet face-to-face, configuration management tools are critical to OSS. Since feedback and contributions can come from anywhere at anytime, project leaders would be occupied full-time in coordination issues if tool support were not available, and indeed, the greatest problem in OSS projects is reckoned to be the bottleneck posed by the lead developers who have to moderate or coordinate the contributions.

By far the most common tool used for configuration management is the CVS (Concurrent Versions System), itself an OSS product (Fogel, 1999). CVS is very well suited to the OSS style of work. Incorporating changes to the repository is very easy, and developers can have anonymous read-only access to the repository. With a single command, developers can download the latest version of the software tree, which is absolutely critical when a large number of developers are working in parallel with no formal division of labor. CVS is the tool used by Apache, GNOME, FreeBSD,

Postgres SQL, and Xemacs (among others), and by the majority of projects hosted at SourceForge. Interestingly, CVS has been criticized for its lack of sophisticated configuration management functionality. Indeed, it has been estimated to be 10 years behind commercial configuration management products (Wilson, 1999).

Fogel (1999) provides a detailed account of the emergence and evolution of CVS. Its roots are in the Unix utility **diff**, which identifies the precise differences between different versions of a module. The output of **diff** can be readily analyzed by the naked eye, and its structured format also allows it to be easily analyzed by means of a computer program. In due course, Larry Wall (of Perl fame) created the **patch** utility which complemented **diff** to the extent that, given any one of a pair of modules and the **diff** output from them, **patch** can re-create the other module.

While these utilities were useful, software development often requires a history of previous versions so that a non-corrupt module can be restored from a previous version. A free software product that fulfilled this need was Revision Control System, written by Walter Tichy. This needed some extra functionality in terms of easy identification of related files, repository locking, and networking. These features were added in the initial version of CVS in 1986, and the product has evolved over the intervening years (Fogel, 1999). The Mozilla Project, for example, recently developed some web-based extensions to complement CVS, including Bugzilla (web-based bug tracking), Bonsai (web-based access to archived source code), and Tinderbox (web-based tools for analyzing software builds) (Cubranic, 1999). CVS poses some interesting questions. If it is lacking in functionality, and is used so frequently by so many, why is no one "itching" to improve it?[4] Likewise, would it be acceptable for OSS developers to use a proprietary, closed configuration management tool to create OSS software?

---

[4] It is worth noting that there is at least one alternative to CVS in production, "Subversion," being developed by Tigris.org (see http://subversion.tigris.org).

However, while CVS might be the most mission-critical OSS tool, a variety of other OSS tools are also available to OSS developers.[5] Bittman *et al.* (2001) have investigated a number of tools for OSS Java development, and rated their usefulness. Their findings suggest that the most useful tools included:

- the Emacs and Gvim text editors for creating and editing source code (Emacs quite easily scales up to a full Java IDE (Travis, 2001));

- the GNU Make and Jakarta ANT build systems;

- Junit for creating a test harness for Java applications;

- Jpython for creating replay scripts and automating GUI usage;

- Jrefactory for restructuring Java code;

- Doc++ for extracting documentation from C , C++, and Java code, and Javadoc for extracting documentation from Java code.

Bittman *et al.* evaluate a number of other OSS tools but conclude that they are less useful and of lower quality than those listed above. Interestingly, these latter, less useful tools cater for the analysis and design phases of software development. Given that these are all OSS tools, the fact that they remain quite underdeveloped suggests that the desire for support for analysis and design does not really coincide with the itches of many OSS developers, as discussed in Chapter 5.

Taboos and norms in OSS development

Formalized project management, in the conventional software engineering sense, does not typically apply in OSS development. Because the development pool spans great geographic and cultural space, face-to-face "meetings" are rare. Furthermore, in non-

---

[5] Given that OSS developers are often working in traditional software development environments, it is reasonable to assume that they use all the tools available in those environments.

commercial OSS development (the majority) there is no organizational bottom-line to consider; nor are there any sanctions in terms of the possibility of firing developers.

However, to avoid chaos, there are some cultural norms that govern how OSS projects are managed. Some of these are in the form of taboos. Chief among these is probably the desire to avoid projects splitting into rival and competing development streams, termed forking in the OSS community (Raymond, 2001HtN). The rationale for the desire to avoid forking is clear, as contributors cannot realistically contribute to multiple forks of the same product simultaneously. Also, even with a large development pool, this is extremely wasteful (note: forking is different to the parallel development phenomenon of competition among solutions as described above). Since the OSS culture is driven by a reputation model (see Chapter 9), the temptation for forking must always be high. For example, one gets most attention from being the project leader, and thus contributing to a project someone else leads is always contributing more to someone else's reputation than one's own. This is not altogether palatable in an ego-based economy.

Another OSS taboo relates to plagiarizing work as one's own by removing the credit to the rightful contributors. This recognition of developer contribution at the micro level of individual modules is vital to ensure that developers are motivated to continue contributing – it represents rapid feedback that one's contribution is valued, and this type of rapid recognition generally does not occur in a traditional software development environment. Likewise, at a macro level, the whole OSS concept is premised on the assumption that pirate developers or organizations will not simply steal the source code that has been made available to them, and convert it to a proprietary closed source product. Thus, hijacking the work of others is a very serious taboo in OSS. Jorgensen (2001) discusses the importance of this in the FreeBSD Project where maintenance responsibility for modules is typically the responsibility of a single individual listed in the log file. The FreeBSD community have enshrined this principle as a rule, "Respect existing maintainers if listed" (FreeBSD, 2001).

Another norm that appears to be very important in the OSS community is modesty and self-deprecation on the part of developers. This is vital if contributions from others are to be solicited. If the original developer conveys the impression that no help is needed, then contributions are not likely to be very forthcoming. There are many examples of this phenomenon in OSS. From the outset, Torvalds' message on August 25, 1991, seeking volunteers to help with Linux development, is the essence of humility:

Hello everybody out there using minix – I'm doing a (free) operating system (just a hobby, won't be big and professional like gnu) for 386 (486) AT clones. This has been brewing since April, and is starting to get ready. I'd like any feedback on things people like/dislike in minix, as my OS resembles it somewhat (same physical layout of the file-system (due to practical reasons) among other things).

I've currently ported bash (1.08) and gcc (1.40), and things seem to work. This implies that I'll get something practical within a few months, and I'd like to know what features most people would want. Any suggestions are welcome, but I won't promise I'll implement them :-)

Linus (torvalds@kruuna.helsinki.fi)

PS. Yes – it's free of any minix code, and it has a multi-threaded fs. It is NOT portable (uses 386 task switching etc), and it probably never will support anything other than AT-harddisks, as that's all I have :-(

Bergquist and Ljungberg (2001) investigate the norms in OSS in some detail. They identify a particular netiquette which is in line with the above by studying postings on a Usenet Linux News Group called *alt.Linux*. In the particular example chosen, a question is submitted by Darren who wants to install Linux on his computer and wants some advice from the community on which distribution to choose:

A Linux Newbie
Umm hello, before I get to my point I'd like to say that I'm pretty new to newsgroups in general and much newer to the linux community, so

please forgive any mistakes I make and if I offend point it out to me and I will be more than happy to say that I am sorry.

Now with that out of the way I'd like to ask anyone who feels like giving an opinion on what distribution of Linux I should get. I am a first time user of Linux but I have used Windows since Windows95 and I have done work in DOS (I am proficient in DOS but hardly fluent). I am currently considering using linux because I hate having to reboot my P2 450 10 times a day just to get Direct X to work properly. To this end I have set aside a little under 4 gigs of hard drive space for Linux. I am currently considering Red Hat, Caldera, or SuSE. Any opinions? Comments? Reasons to have me committed? ;)

Now if you are going to reply to this (hey it could happen) can I convince anyone to send me an E-mail directly as opposed to just posting to the group? Outlook Express 5 is pretty damn flighty and I don't want to risk losing a valuable opinion. If you would prefer replying to the group that is fine, I am just stating a loose preference.

Also as I am Completely new to linux I was wondering if anyone could recommend a good book on it? maybe on linux in general and the packages I mentioned before?

Good lordy this is a long post I hope no-one flames me...
Thank you for your time and I hope I haven't earned your malice

Sincerely,
Darren

In a very rich and detailed analysis of this individual message, Bergquist and Ljungberg identify a complex set of norm-governed practices. They point to the fact that Darren overstates his newness to newsgroups, as he is actually familiar with some of the basic rules for interacting there. He also reveals a modesty in relation to his expertise in DOS. Yet, he exhibits a clear grasp of the relevant technical issues – e.g., how much disk space he has available, and also the vagaries of Outlook Express 5, clearly identifying the version number (mentioning the frailty of a Microsoft product would probably not do him any harm in this community either). He may elicit the sympathy of the community with his stated frustration with the constant reboots. Thus, his desire to install Linux is not based on an idealistic whim – he is no Johnny-come-lately academic jumping on the bandwagon (note that neither of the authors of this book is called Johnny). Overall, Darren exhibits a quite sophisticated awareness. He wants to keep his posting short to avoid flaming, and pretends that a response ("hey it could happen") is unexpected. But his queries are a model in conciseness and clarity. Perhaps, the bottom line is that he gets a reply from Leonard 20 minutes later (also reported by Bergquist and Ljungberg):

Re: A Linux Newbie
Well Darren, I think you did ok…
you didn't post in HTML
you didn't cross-post
you didn't post a binary
you weren't a jerk and were generally polite…

I'm going to assume you took the time to catch up with the newsgroup before posting to make sure your question hasn't been answered so all proper nettiqite (sp?) has been obeyed. How nice….

I used Redhat Linux 5.2 when I got started. If I was starting today I would buy the 6.0 or more likely the Mandrake as it is the same stuff for 1/3 the price…and I hear it's easier to install.

The learning curve is mighty steep at first, but it gets better and you'll wonder why you waited so long.

As far as books, I found "Mastering Linux" to be basic, outdated and at times inaccurate…and it was far too reliant on the X interface. I actually found the "Linux for Dummies" book had exactly the same information in much less space, and therefore was much more helpful (despite the title and the stigma attached to it) and dealt more with the command line. I'm looking for a good intermediate book now….

Good luck
Leonard

It is worth noting that, in his message, before dealing with the substance of the query, Leonard chooses to deal with issues of netiquette (even if his spelling of the word is, as he acknowledges, very approximate indeed). This further reinforces the importance of the norms to ensure that time is not wasted, and the low threshold of tolerance to noise is obvious. Bergquist and Ljunberg also report evidence that this is very much the case in the following email extract:

Giving Back

siberian – April 01st 1999, 21:31 EST

More then once I have had the urge to begin contributing to the community. I have written code, documented it and gained authorization for its release. But at the last minute I always hesitate and then stop. Why? I think I fear the fangs of the community. At this point, everywhere I turn its a big flamefest and getting quite tiresome. Its gotten to the point where it seems one has to be some sort of Jedi Master level coder to contribute. On more then a few mailing lists I have seen contributors flamed for their contributions! Flaming someone for GIVING something away. Its incredible.

Given the esoteric nature of the OSS community where behavior is governed by these norms which are not always explicitly documented, the *rites de passage* initiation into the community often requires an intimate familiarity with these esoteric norms and conventions – a classic "Catch-22" situation. Raymond (2001HtN) cites the example of the Usenet newsgroup, alt.sysadmin.recovery, which requires knowledge of a specific secret before one can post. However, the secret is not documented anywhere and members are loath to reveal it. In a similar fashion, Jorgensen (2001) identifies this as a part of the FreeBSD culture where achieving committer-level status requires the modification of one's entry in the CVS log by adding oneself to the "Developers" section and removing the entry from the "Additional Contributors" section, seen as "a relatively easy task, but...a good first test of your CVS skills" (FreeBSD, 2001). Interestingly, the norms are actually quite well documented for some projects, e.g., FreeBSD (FreeBSD, 2001), Apache HTTP Project (Apache Software Foundation, 2001b), and Mozilla (Mozilla

Organization, 2001). Given the distributed nature of the OSS development pool, these well-defined guidelines for the submission of contributions, coding style, tests, etc., are very useful.

The OSS development life cycle

The traditional software development life cycle (SDLC) is premised on a set of stages, which, in their most generic form, include

- planning;

- analysis;

- design;

- implementation.

However, the OSS development life cycle is quite different. Firstly, the planning, analysis, and design phases are largely conducted by the initial project founder, and are not part of the general OSS development life cycle. As will be discussed in Chapter 10, getting design issues right is perhaps even more critical in OSS than in conventional development. Certain criteria in relation to modularity of the code are critical. For example, modules must be loosely coupled, thereby allowing distributed development in the first place. Less important, but still highly desirable for achieving an efficient development model, is that modules be highly cohesive and address a single well-defined purpose. However, design decisions are generally made in advance, before the larger pool of developers start to contribute, and are generally based on well-established design patterns. This allows developers to collaborate without having to undergo the detailed requirements analysis or design phases of the traditional life cycle. In the absence of conventional project management, the importance of "having a tail-light to follow" (Bezroukov, 1999b) is a very useful coordinating principle, as it allows a multitude of developers to contribute.

This also helps to explain why many OSS products are horizontal infrastructure-type products, as these are ones in which the requirements are pretty well understood. In vertical domains, developer knowledge of the application domain has been found to be critical, but it is unlikely that the pool of potential developers would be as high in such domains. This issue is discussed in detail in Chapter 10.

Thus, the OSS development life cycle is located primarily within the implementation phase of the traditional SDLC. Several researchers have investigated the life cycle underpinning OSS. Bollinger *et al.* (1999) suggest that it follows a very intensive spiral model (Boehm, 1988), albeit without any real risk assessment. Mockus *et al.* (2000) have derived a life cycle for OSS from their study of the Apache Project, and Jorgensen (2001) has investigated the life cycle in the FreeBSD Project. Both have come up with models that are largely compatible, but Jorgensen's is more detailed. He identifies the following main phases in the OSS development life cycle:

Code
　⇒Review
　　⇒Pre-commit test
　　　⇒Development release
　　　　⇒Parallel debugging
　　　　　⇒Production release

Code

This is the *sine qua non* activity. However, many potential OSS contributors may fear taking the initial step of submitting their code for review by the supremely talented OSS "code-gods" (Asklund and Bendix, 2001; Bergquist and Ljungberg, 2001), a fear that is quite warranted when one considers the views of a FreeBSD developer reported by Jorgensen (2001):

> The way you get commit privileges is by first making enough code contributions…This implies the code you've been submitting is of sufficiently impressive quality that no one objects and says, "Yuck, no, don't give him commit privileges. He writes ugly code."

Thus, the knowledge that talented and respected peers will be reviewing the code is a real incentive to improve the quality of the code being submitted in the first place.

Review

As already mentioned, truly independent peer review is one of the central strengths of the OSS process. However, Jorgensen found that eliciting feedback was not always easy. "Heavyweights" with a proven reputation will get a lot of feedback, but it can be quite difficult to get attention as a newbie – another classic "Catch-22" situation. Also, somewhat paradoxically, the simpler the code, the more feedback one gets. However, complex code would invariably benefit more from feedback. Also, it is more difficult to get feedback on design issues.

Pre-commit test

Given the vulnerability of the OSS development model, it is critical that committers test each contribution carefully to avoid breaking the build, another common norm in the OSS community. Since there is no convenient help-line or telephone support for those installing the eventual product, it can be an adventure in itself completing an actual OSS product installation. Sanders (1998) quotes the "tech-savvy" Ellen Ullman's description of her installation of Linux as "an exhilarating succession of problem-solving challenges." Given this problematic installation context, it is imperative that installation proceeds as smoothly as possible without unnecessary noise, and thus rogue modules which could jeopardize this must be prevented.

Interestingly, testing is very much a personal process. There is no requirement that test scenarios be rigorously planned and written down in advance. However, the negative implications of allowing a faulty contribution through are such that the testing process is taken very seriously indeed. As mentioned above, the delegation of testing to the user community – or partial delegation, as is the case with Mozilla and GNOME – is one of the strengths of OSS (Schmidt and Porter, 2001).

Development release

If the committer deems the module ready, it can be incorporated in the development release. This is the key payoff for many developers as they get the reward of seeing their code implemented quickly in the product. Jorgensen (2001) cites a developer who captures it quite graphically:

> There is a tremendous satisfaction to the "see bug, fix bug, see bug fix get incorporated so that the fix helps others" cycle.

Parallel debugging

The advantages of global parallel debugging were discussed above. Again, as in testing, there is typically no formal plan for debugging. Rather the numbers of potential debuggers is where the power of the debugging arises – Linus's Law. If bugs are found, they can be fixed and re-submitted as per the life cycle described above, or problem reports may be created and submitted. This can also be a way of initiating one's contribution to OSS. For example, the database of outstanding problem reports could be examined, and if there are some outstanding that catch one's interest or are within one's capability, then these can be worked on. Thus, can one begin a career in OSS.

Production release

Contributions eventually become part of the production release. They are merged into the stable production branch. This is accomplished in different ways in different projects. FreeBSD maintains stable production and current development branches, and contributions that are eventually found suitable are merged into the latest stable production branch, and, in the case of a bug fix, to any previous production branches to which it might be relevant. Linux maintains its stable production and development versions in different directories, and uses release numbers to identify production (even numbers) and development (odd numbers) versions.

Conclusion

Above, we have argued that the generic OSS development process is characterized by the practice of parallel, rather than linear, collaboration among developers, which leads to increases in both speed and quality; by the participation of large, globally distributed communities of developers who participate in a truly independent peer review process; by prompt feedback (e.g., bug reports) and prompt recognition (e.g., integration of bug fixes); by the participation of talented and motivated developers and extremely active users; and by rapid, incremental release schedules. We also examined the well-stocked toolkit of OSS, including configuration management tools like CVS, as well as editors, build tools, documentation extractors, and the like. Finally, we argued that the OSS process is governed by an elaborate system of taboos and social mores which take the place of formal project management, and that the OSS process follows a distinctly different development life cycle to traditional proprietary software.

7

Stakeholders: who are the developers and organizations involved?

In this chapter, we explore our third analytical category, stakeholders. We identify four major groups involved in OSS (developer communities, user communities, commercial and non-commercial organizations), discuss the distinguishing characteristics of each group, and examine how each group performs in the various roles of client, actor, and owner.

OSS stakeholders

Within the OSS domain, we can identify at least four major groups of stakeholders: developer communities, user communities, commercial and non-commercial organizations. These groups, of course, are far from mutually exclusive. Many OSS users are also developers, and it can be argued that all OSS developers are also users. Likewise, commercial and non-commercial organizations both use and develop OSS products, as well as serving other functions such as advocacy and support. Below, we seek to identify the distinguishing characteristics of each group and examine the ways in which each of these groups act at different times as clients (beneficiaries), actors (agents of change), and owners (decision makers).

OSS developer communities

The truth is, we don't know very much about the demographics of OSS developers – this is in fact one of the major gaps in the OSS research domain. As already mentioned, estimates of the number of developers involved in OSS vary a great deal. For example, Raymond (2001CatB) has suggested that more than 40,000 people have collaborated on Linux alone, and when challenged on this figure recently,[1] revised the estimate up to 750,000 contributors, whereas Markus *et al.* (2000) estimate the total number of OSS developers on all projects to be 750,000. McConnell (1999) arrives at a more sober estimate of 1,200 Linux developers, although Torvalds himself suggests that Linux development comprises "hundreds of thousands of developers" (Torvalds and Diamond, 2001). Clearly, more rigorous research is needed in this area. Nonetheless, enough research has been done to draw some preliminary conclusions about the OSS development community.

One of the most demographically rich studies to date took place in April 2000, when a group of researchers in Germany surveyed 142 members (from 28 different countries) of a Linux kernel development mailing list. The purpose of the study was to better understand the motivations of individual kernel developers – a topic which we return to in Chapter 9 – but a certain amount of descriptive information was also collected and analyzed. The majority of participants in *The Linux Study*, as it came to be called, were male (~96 percent), between the ages of 20 and 39 (~70 percent), and lived in the United States (~45 percent) or Europe (~40 percent) (Hermann *et al.* 2000; Niedner *et al.* 2000). As a single study of a single developer community, it goes without saying that this portrait needs to be validated through further research. Nonetheless, the data is potentially significant. For example, the age range of the participants points to developers who are at the junior to mid-career

---

[1] Keynote address by Eric Raymond to IFIP WG8.2 conference (Russo *et al.*, 2001) in Boise, Idaho, July 28, 2001.

level – this is a direct contradiction to the popular misconception of the teen-hacker-in-the-bedroom. Examining the raw data (Niedner, 2000), we come across three interesting trends:

- *Most of the participants are relative newcomers to the Linux kernel development community*. Around 60 percent had been involved for a year or less, and around 18 percent had been involved between one and two years. Although the relationship between the two events is not established, this indicates growth in the kernel developer community coinciding with the coining of the term Open Source and the subsequent increase in OSS's public profile. Only three participants indicated involvement in the 7–8-year range, which would identify them as members of the earliest kernel development community.

- *Participants tended to be specialists*. Around 85 percent worked on only one or two kernel subprojects, and only six participants reported working on more than four subprojects.

- *Participants tended to be professionals.* Around 18 percent claimed to receive regular payment for their kernel development work, and a further 18 percent claimed to receive occasional payment. Around 65 percent were employed full-time and about 32 percent reported that they did most of their development during working, rather than leisure hours.

Another, much larger study carried out by members of the *UNC Open Source Research Team* revealed similar findings to those above. This study was based on the contents of the *UNC MetaLab Linux Archives* (formerly *Sunsite*), one of the oldest and largest repositories of Linux software. In particular, the study focused on application, rather than kernel-level software, thus providing a complementary picture to *The Linux Study* discussed above. The only demographic data gathered in the *UNC MetaLab* study was geographic in nature – namely that 37 percent of the software authors in the *Archives* used European email suffixes, while 52 percent used US top-level domains (.com, .edu., .net, and .org).

Assuming that some of the .com addresses are used by individuals in Europe, we see a similar geographic distribution to that found in the kernel study. Like *The Linux Study*, the *UNC MetaLab* study demonstrates a steady increase in development activity in recent years (i.e., since the coining of the term Open Source). Nearly 48 percent of the additions and changes made in the archives were made in 1998 and 1999, over half of those made in the six months preceding the study! The *UNC MetaLab* study also seems to support the idea that OSS developers tend to be specialists. Over 90 percent of software authors had made only one or two additions or changes to the archives, and only half of 1 percent had made more than 10 additions/changes (Dempsey *et al.*, 1999).

Unfortunately, the *UNC MetaLab* study can offer no further evidence for, or against, the notion that OSS developers tend to be professionals. However, there is evidence to be found elsewhere. For example, of the 62 members of the Apache Software Foundation, at least 40 are affiliated with software companies (Apache Software Foundation, 2001e), and a similar ratio can be found in the Apache HTTP Server core group (Apache Software Foundation, 2000). A study of the FreeBSD Project also showed that nearly half of the developers were paid by their employers for their OSS-related work (Jorgensen, 2001). However, the above evidence has to be qualified somewhat, since the study by Koch and Schneider (2001) of the GNOME Project reported a usage pattern that would suggest that many OSS developers do contribute irregularly and in their spare time.

Thus, while we do not have much demographic information, we do find enough descriptive data to argue that OSS developers tend to be professionals and specialists, both significant characteristics. If the majority of OSS developers (or at least core developers) tend to be professionals and specialists, this helps to explain how the largely uncoordinated efforts of individual developers can lead to software that is highly robust (Jorgensen, 2001; Neumann, 1998, 2000a, 2000b). As professionals, it is reasonable to assume that individual developers are bringing industry best practices to bear on OSS problems. Likewise, as specialists, individual developers are likely to possess significant passion for the subject matter, further supporting the production of elegant and efficient applications and components (Raymond, 2001). The specialist status of OSS developers is important for another reason as well. Specialization makes possible task decomposition, modularity, and parallel development, all critical aspects of the OSS process, as discussed in previous chapters (cf. Moon and Sproull, 2000; Koch and Schneider, 2001).

OSS developers, both as individuals and communities, regularly shift between the roles of client, actor, and owner – and the distinctions between these roles are often blurred. There is ample evidence that OSS developers are clients – that is to say beneficiaries – of OSS, as they are by far the most regular users of OSS products. As discussed previously, OSS developers (almost religiously) use OSS products (CVS, GNU Emacs, GCC, etc.) to support the development process itself, and looking at the programming languages being used in OSS development (see Chapter 1) we find little evidence of OSS development taking place using non-OSS tools. Furthermore, we find a tendency in large OSS projects, like the Linux kernel, towards running two parallel release structures, one for stable use and one for innovation, which supports a "bootstrapping" mode of operation (building Linux on Linux) common to OSS.

Just as in a traditional systems development environment, OSS developers are primarily agents of change; in other words, the system's "actors." However, there are really two developer–actor roles within OSS. The first role might be termed "re-actor" and refers to an agent making changes in order to repair reported defects in the software. The re-actor role can be seen as existing on the edge between actor and client – minor changes made in direct response to the client experience. The second role is that of "pro-actor," an agent making changes in order to contribute new functionality. The pro-actor role falls closer to the actor-owner boundary, and in some cases we find that the individuals and groups who ultimately implement changes to a system have such a high level of authority (e.g., Torvalds for Linux or The Perl Porters Group for Perl) that they are simultaneously acting as the software's owner. An analysis of these roles in the Apache HTTP Server Project (Mockus *et al.*, 2000) supports this distinction, showing that while the core group of developers spent the bulk of their development time in the role of pro-actor, the wider development community assumed the role of re-actor, focusing on the smaller projects involved in maintenance and defect repair.

Although we can say that the primary author(s) or maintainer(s) of an OSS product act as the product's owner, the owner role in OSS is never as absolute or exclusive as it is in the proprietary software world. In Chapter 4, we defined two aspects of the owner role – prime concern for the system and the ultimate power in relation to whether the system continues to exist. There are certainly groups and individuals who exhibit "prime concern for the system" (for example, The Python Software Foundation for the ongoing evolution of Python), and these groups make use of several tools to maintain control over the direction of an OSS project (legal protection of project names, access-control over the "official" release version, etc.). However, we do not see individuals or groups who can claim ultimate power in relation to whether the system continues to exist. In fact, one of the key benefits to the OSS process is the capacity for software to survive a "change of cast." If the current "owner" ceases to be involved, another owner will step up to bat – assuming the software remains useful to the community (see, for example, Borland, 2000). It is true that the author of OSS software can fork the project and release new versions of the software under a closed license, at which point they can effect the immediate demise of this new, proprietary software. However, as long as a product remains OSS, there is no way for any "owner," author or not, to unilaterally cause that product to cease to exist.

OSS user communities

Again, as with OSS developers, demographic profiles of OSS users are scarce. Nevertheless, we have enough evidence to identify a few general trends and characteristics.

In terms of the global OSS user community, some interesting trends on accessibility have been discovered. Wang and Whitehead

(2001) found that while the ratio of Apache sites to Microsoft's Internet Information Services (IIS) server is 3:1 over all domains, the ratio drops to 1:1 in non-English-speaking countries. They attribute this to the superior internationalization and localization of IIS. Thus, the OSS movement clearly has some way to go in these areas, but they should not present a significant problem for OSS developers and users, although it seems to be the case that internationalization and localization are more difficult to achieve if they are not factored into the original design.

OSS products like Linux have enjoyed a much higher adoption rate in the corporate computing market than in the personal computing market, where one or another version of Microsoft Windows is still shipping on around 9 out of every 10 machines (Shankland, 2001). We use the term "shipping" rather than "running" to highlight the primary problem with counting home Linux users – namely that most users install Linux on a machine which already contained a factory install of a Windows operating system, a practice which led to the now legendary 1999 "Windows Refund Day" demonstration.[2]

Within the corporate computing market, we see more businesses exploiting OSS products in their back-end systems – particularly Internet systems – than in their desktop environments. Part of this is due to the fact that OSS server software like Apache, BIND, and Sendmail dramatically outperform their proprietary competition. Another factor is the historical lack of OSS office productivity software, and the perception (whether valid or not) that OSS cannot deliver a desktop computing environment for the non-specialist.[3]

The same holds true in the personal computing market. Individuals directly using OSS products at home have traditionally consisted of "early adopters," users embracing technology ahead of the mainstream market. This user community overlaps significantly

---

[2] See http://uncle-enzo.linuxmafia.com/refund/
[3] As we've noted previously, desktop environment projects like GNOME and KDE, and office suites like OpenOffice and GNOME Office are maturing and may signal a change in this situation in the near future.

with the developer community, and enjoys the power OSS gives them to engage in highly expert activities (development, customization, etc.), activities often more similar to back-end system administration than to general desktop computing. It can also be argued that the non-expert OSS user community is using OSS second-hand and unaware of the fact. For example, individuals who regularly use web services like Yahoo! Mail or Amazon Recommendations (a staggeringly large group) are in fact using software services produced on an OSS platform. An additional characteristic of non-corporate OSS user communities is the high level of activity surrounding knowledge transfer among users. The same tools used by OSS developers – the web, email, bulletin boards, etc. – are regularly used by OSS users to support their individual computing activities.

The profile of Open Source Software, and of OSS users, is changing and will continue to change. Massive efforts are being made to produce user-friendly desktop environments (GNOME, KDE) as well as to produce standard end-user applications. Raymond (2001) has repeatedly predicted the adoption of Linux on the desktop, an event he sees tied to the falling price of hardware and the need for original equipment manufacturers (OEMs) to maintain margins. While other industry analysts concur with Raymond's predictions, some, notably Tim O'Reilly, have questioned whether or not the desktop battle is really worth fighting. O'Reilly (in Goth, 2001) states:

> Public rhetoric has focused so much on the battle that people haven't seen how much Open Source has been the leader the past five years. ... When you have an overwhelming advantage in the next generation of applications, why would you want to go backwards? ... Microsoft [with initiatives like .Net] are still imitating the Open Source community while the Open Source community is now imitating Microsoft – which is stupid. ... In fact, Open Source software had a real lead on the Web. The Apache Group is continuing to do a lot of forward-looking work. They just don't get that much attention.

Certainly, we continue to see a certain inertia favoring systems software and development tools over end-user applications (see

Chapter 1). We also see commercial interest in funding the OSS desktop war growing comparatively slowly, although there are exceptions (e.g., Sun Microsystems). Notably, in May 2001, Eazel, a highly visible commercial OSS desktop development house, announced its bankruptcy.

We turn now to the roles that the members of OSS user communities play. Primarily, we see users acting in the role of client. Frequently, the individual in question is directly using and benefiting from the software product, for example an Apache administrator setting up a new domain. Sometimes, as mentioned above, the user is indirectly using and benefiting from the product, for example a consumer checking the status of their Amazon order using Internet Explorer on Windows 98.

It is possible to treat an OSS product like a "black box" or a commercial, off-the-shelf product (Hissam and Weinstock, 2001). However, unlike most of their proprietary counterparts, OSS users also have the option of directly effecting change in the system, in other words becoming actors. User–actors engage in activities like submitting bug reports, suggesting new functionality, participating in the conversations of the development community, creating documentation, etc. (cf. Lakhani and von Hippel, 2000).

Finally, unlike any of their proprietary counterparts, OSS users can be said to be true owners of their software – not simply licensed users. While the user of a product like GNU Emacs cannot assume ownership of the credit for developing the program, he or she can enjoy all of the freedoms and powers associated with ownership distribution, modification, etc.

OSS commercial organizations

In this section we look at three companies – IBM, Red Hat, and Cosource – whose activities are representative of the commercial OSS world. We use these companies to outline the basic characteristics of OSS companies, and then discuss the roles of client, actor, and owner.

IBM is one of the most active proprietary-OSS hybrid companies. IBM is, of course, a major OEM, and like many other OEMs – Atipa, Compaq, Dell, Gateway, Penguin Computing, etc. – IBM builds and sells complete Linux systems. System vending – which amounts to selling the hardware and giving the software away at negligible cost – is the primary OSS business model for OEMs. Other OEM activities include the production of OSS device drivers, the optimization of OSS products for particular platforms, etc. But IBM is more than an OEM; it is also an independent software vendor (ISV). Like many proprietary ISVs (Corel, Oracle, etc.), IBM has ported their proprietary software – WebSphere (which incorporates Apache technology), Lotus, DB2, Domino, etc. – to the Linux platform. "Linux-enabling" existing software is a major ISV business model. Interestingly, while the OSI welcomes this kind of activity (the more high-quality applications available for OSS operating systems, the better), the FSF sometimes sees this as nothing more than an exploitation of the OSS market. Regarding Apple's forays into Free Software, Stallman (2001b) wrote:

> Overall, I think that Apple's action is an example of the effects of the year-old "open source" movement: of its plan to appeal to business with the purely materialistic goal of faster development, while putting aside the deeper issues of freedom, community, cooperation, and what kind of society we want to live in.
>
> Apple has grasped perfectly the concept with which "open source" is promoted, which is a "show users the source and they will help you fix bugs". What Apple has not grasped – or has dismissed – is the spirit of free software, which is that we form a community to cooperate on the commons of software.

In addition to selling hardware and software, IBM is also generating revenue by providing technical support and training services, including Red Hat Certification courses. Support and training represent probably the most substantial OSS business opportunity (the majority of Red Hat's revenue comes from support and training) since margins on selling OSS products are so small.

IBM is also supporting the OSS community, and gaining important mind-share, by offering free, online training for various OSS technologies.

Internally, IBM is at least partially emulating the OSS process. IBM's *alphaWorks* program makes emergent technologies available with source code, thus involving the wider development–user community at the earliest stages of product development. Much of this technology becomes proprietary at the end of the day, while some remains OSS (see below). This kind of pseudo-OSS development is being experimented with in a number of companies, for example HP (Dinkelacker and Garg, 2001), Netscape (Hecker, 1999; Lewis, 1999), and Apple.[4]

Finally, IBM plays host and lead developer for a number of software projects at the *developerWorks* website, using OSI-certified licenses (primarily the IBM Public License). IBM, like Sun Microsystems, has also been heavily involved in a number of projects run by the *Apache Software Foundation*, and is one of the sponsors of the *Linux Internationalization Initiative*. On the one hand, IBM is producing software to become a recognized member of the OSS community. This is an important and common business practice in its own right. On the other hand, IBM's participation as a developer of OSS software can also be seen as part of a platform war. For example, IBM has been most active in supporting the Apache XML Project. This project is in many ways running a dead-heat race with companies like Microsoft to develop the *de facto* XML toolkit. More importantly, the Apache Project seeks to ensure that W3C standards – like XML Schema Definition Language – are adopted, rather than proprietary technologies like Microsoft's XML-Data Reduced schema language, thus avoiding the fate that HTML suffered in the past.

We turn now to a pure-play OSS company, namely Red Hat. First of all, it should be noted that Red Hat's status as a pure-play is starting to come into question. Until recently, Red Hat exclusively sold OSS software, but that is no longer the case. Now you can buy

---

[4] http://www.darwin.org/

Red Hat Linux bundled with proprietary software packages like IBM's DB2, Lotus, and WebSphere. Red Hat also sells the Stronghold Secure Web Server, which contains proprietary software even though the Apache HTTP Server is at the core. Nonetheless, we chose to treat Red Hat as a pure-play OSS organization, since that is how they started and that is the business sector they best represent.

As we noted in Chapter 3, Red Hat is the most successful Linux distributor in the corporate market, competing with companies like Caldera, Suse, and Linux Mandrake. Although Red Hat and other Linux distributors develop a certain amount of software (such as the Red Hat Package Manager), companies like Red Hat are not primarily ISVs, rather they can be characterized as value added resellers (VARs) with an unorthodox ISV (the OSS community) supplying the software. Red Hat sells a wide variety of products, including various configurations of the Linux OS and development tool kits like GNUPro (added to the catalog when Red Hat bought Cygnus). As a retailer, Red Hat adds value primarily as an integration specialist – testing and optimizing configurations for various tasks.

As we noted above, Red Hat makes the bulk of its money not from the low-margin sale of OSS products, but from the high-margin sale of support and training services. Red Hat is primarily in the "trusted brand" business, and has embraced whole-heartedly Raymond's (2001) idea that software is a service industry operating under the illusion that it is a manufacturing industry (Young, 1999; Young and Rohm, 1999). At the low end of the scale, a consumer or business might choose to purchase an official Red Hat distribution rather than an identical and even cheaper unofficial distribution, because of the comfort and peace of mind associated with Red Hat's guarantee and installation support. Red Hat support services scale up from there into an extremely lucrative suite of packages.

Red Hat also sells training and certification services (which they call Learning Services). The RHCE (Red Hat Certified Engineer) Program is the flagship of the Red Hat offering, but training is also available for developers, eBusiness professionals, and for embedded systems professionals. Finally, Red Hat runs a vibrant marketplace for hardware, software, hosting and consulting services through the

"Red Hat Marketplace" network of vendors and various partner programs.

Above, we looked at how Red Hat generates revenue. We turn now to the more important question of how Red Hat maintains its relationship with the development community that made this revenue possible. Red Hat has had its share of bad PR days, for example when Red Hat offered 5,000 OSS developers an opportunity to participate in its IPO, and only 1,150 of the 1,300 who wanted to were able to buy stock at the original price of $14 – the other 150 were turned down (Kanellos and Shankland, 1999). Red Hat has made a quiet discipline out of feeding revenue back into OSS, for example the royalties for Young and Rohm's (1999) book, *Under the Radar*, go to the GNU Project. Red Hat has also done much to support the OSS community in terms of producing OSS products, hosting projects, creating documentation, and hosting discussion forums and knowledge bases.

Our last OSS company, Cosource, is very different from IBM and Red Hat. Cosource, which we discussed in Chapter 5, has made a business model out of the OSS process, rather than out of an OSS product. Cosource hosts a reverse-auction that enables consumers and developers of OSS products to work together to fund the development of various software solutions. Cosource consumers post requests for new OSS packages, extensions, or in some cases, documentation and training. Cosource developers then submit proposals to develop the package (including price and schedule) and name an "Authority," or third-party peer reviewer. Cosource consumers (not just the ones who post the initial request) may then elect to commit funds to one or more of the project proposals. The first proposal which reaches full funding enters development. The third-party peer reviewer, or Authority, declares when the project is complete, and it is then released. The participating consumers pay their commitments via credit card, and the developer and Authority are also paid for their work (less a percentage for Cosource). The overall Cosource business model is based on bringing the advantage of using OSS products (the ability to modify the software) into reach for companies without technical expertise who would otherwise be treating the OSS product as a black box. Furthermore, since multiple consumers can fund projects, the cost of development is shared. Cosource is wooing the development community by marketing benefits like the opportunity to gain experience and to potentially earn a living developing OSS products, all without the entrepreneurial overhead of setting up an independent development business. As noted earlier, Cosource's only real competition, Collab.Net's SourceXchange service, ceased operations in April 2001. Collab.Net continues to be a healthy company, and like Cosource, has built a business model around supporting the OSS process.

Based on these three companies, we begin to get a sense of the characteristics of OSS commercial organizations. First, we see that companies are addressing OSS as an important market – not a viable licensing model – and are porting proprietary software to OSS platforms. Though potentially lucrative, we note that this does alienate certain portions of the OSS community. Second, we see that whether as OEMs or VARs, OSS companies are in the value-adding business, providing optimization services, technical support, training, etc. Simply selling OSS products does not necessarily generate enough revenue to sustain a large organization. Third, and most importantly, we see companies seeking to establish a trust-filled relationship with the OSS community. In all three cases, new code is being released into the community, and companies like IBM and Red Hat demonstrate the importance of giving back to the community in the form of information and hosting services as well. It is important to note that these activities serve another purpose as well, for like IBM with XML, many of Red Hat's development efforts can be seen as a form of platform building – expanding the viability of Linux in general, before leaning on the Red Hat brand to capture that expanded market. Finally, we see that the OSS process itself – collaboration, peer review, etc. – becomes the seed for a truly innovative business model, which might be termed "Open Out-Sourcing."

Companies like those discussed above perform generally in client and actor roles. As clients of OSS, we've already discussed the adoption of OSS products by commercial organizations in general, and companies actually in the OSS business are no exception – one would be hard pressed, for example, to find an OSS company website not running Apache. The OSI makes the important observation that OSS companies serve as living examples of the prowess of OSS products – for example, Walnut Creek's FreeBSD-based ftp site which supports up to 5,000 simultaneous user connections. Furthermore, due to the OSS nature of the products, these companies are beneficiaries in another sense, namely they can learn from each other without expensive reverse engineering, thus fueling rapid innovation. Caldera doesn't run Red Hat servers, but they learn from Red Hat releases and vice versa. OSS companies also behave as actors, or agents of change. In some cases, this is an active role – IBM developing Jikes, Red Hat developing the RPM. But companies also act as patrons of change – in the Renaissance sense – effecting change by providing the resources that support change. It is less clear how such companies act as owners of software – as we noted above, it is difficult for any OSS product to have a true owner. Certainly, IBM reserves the power to kill (close) future releases of individual *alphaWorks* software projects, but the code in a Red Hat Linux 7.1 distribution (though not the Red Hat brand) would survive the bankruptcy of the company. Even the control that these companies have over the direction of their products is subtle. Red Hat, for example, has little influence over the development of the Linux kernel, but has tremendous influence over the public perception of what an OSS operating system should be.

OSS non-commercial organizations

Finally, we turn briefly to the fourth stakeholder group, non-profit organizations, many of whose activities we discussed in Chapter 3. Although we separated advocacy groups from project hosts in our previous discussion, it is clear that advocacy is a primary quality in all of these groups. In fact, a passion for the ideology behind OSS seems to be what prevents many of these organizations from becoming profit-earning entities. We also see that most OSS organizations profess themselves to be a meritocracy. While the administrative functions of a legal foundation may be formalized in a board of directors, projects are run – and advanced by – individual developers willing to invest the time and talent. These organizations are also characterized by diversity, and there is an enormous amount of variety in leadership patterns and collaborative strategies between groups. There are some commonalities, though – use of a unifying web presence, recognition for even the smallest contribution, support in the form of hosted conversations and documentation, well-defined contributor style guides, and active bug reporting tools.

Like their commercial counterparts, non-profit groups are regular clients of OSS products, and major projects like Apache, GNOME, and Python can be identified as the ultimate actors in OSS, bringing together as they do the various individual developers involved. These organizations can also be said to be as close to an owner as is possible in OSS – since they grew out of the community, they crystallize, rather than undermine, the community's authority. And, for many of the most popular OSS products, the supporting organizations jealously and successfully guard their right to guide the development of the product – an important prevention against forking and incompatibility.

Conclusion

Above, we examined the characteristics of four stakeholder groups. We saw evidence to suggest that the community of OSS developers has been growing steadily over recent years, and that a large percentage of this community is professional, not amateur. We also argued that OSS developers tend to be specialists, not generalists, which benefits from and perpetuates both the modularity of OSS products and the distributed, parallel nature of the OSS process.

Turning to the user community, we noted the higher level of penetration in the corporate market, and the tendency for these corporate users to exploit OSS for back-office functionality. We characterized private OSS users as early adopters and power users, though we noted that this is changing.

We also discussed the common traits of companies participating in OSS and argued that many companies are not actually embracing OSS, only the possibility of selling existing proprietary software on the Linux platform. Among companies genuinely experimenting with OSS, we see a tendency towards service and support-oriented business models, community-fostering and intensive brand management.

Finally, we examined non-profit organizations, and suggested that they tend towards advocacy as well as software development, organize themselves in terms of merit and level of member participation, and do in fact offer quite a bit of support for project managers, such as style guides and reporting and collaboration.

We also addressed the roles played by each of these four groups. Our analysis is summarized as follows:

▶

	as CLIENT	as ACTOR	as OWNER
Developers	Regularly use OSS products to support development.	Act as the main implementers of changes in systems, both in a proactive and reactive mode.	Exhibit prime concern for the systems direction, but do not necessarily possess the power to terminate the system.
Users	Both directly and indirectly use OSS products.	Can use OSS as a black box, or actually make changes. Can also effect change through bug reports, etc.	Have as much claim to ownership (not authorship) as the creator of the software.
Companies	Have been the most enthusiastic adopters of OSS, and in many cases showcase their use of OSS products.	Act as both implementers and patrons of change.	Assert control over brand and over direction of branded distributions, but not necessarily over actual product.
Non-profit Organizations	Use OSS products *à la* Companies.	Organize developer efforts.	Often assert highest level of control over direction and future of projects.

(The shaded cell indicates the primary role(s) played by the stakeholder group.)

8

Environment: where and when does Open Source development take place?

In this chapter, we explore the environmental aspects of Open Source Software. This corresponds to the geographic and temporal aspects of OSS as presented in the framework derived in Chapter 4, and has antecedents directly in Zachman's (1987) "where" and "when" categories. First, we discuss the various online and offline spaces in which OSS stakeholders interact. Second, we look at temporal aspects of OSS development, distribution, and evolution.

The "where?" of OSS

In previous chapters we have already pointed out that OSS development takes place among distributed teams, that participants can be found (physically) in many different parts of the world, and that they communicate and collaborate primarily in the pseudo-space of the Internet. In this section we take a closer look at the spaces – both online and offline – in which OSS stakeholders interact.

OSS online

OSS stakeholders primarily interact in virtual environments, using Internet tools. Indeed, as we have repeatedly emphasized, the Internet is the primary enabler of the OSS development and distribution process, making it possible for widely distributed groups to share ideas and software extremely quickly at negligible cost. And we have seen evidence (in Chapter 5) that suggests the OSS development community recognizes its dependence on the network – namely the high level of the "scratching-the-personal-itch" type of development activity in the area of Internet software.

Long before the term Open Source was coined (or Free Software for that matter), the developers of the products that would later bear these labels communicated and collaborated regularly through a distributed bulletin board system called Usenet. Probably the most commonly cited product of this environment is the Linux kernel, born in the comp.os.minix Usenet newsgroup, but there are certainly many others. Usenet began in 1979, the work of four individuals – Steve Bellovin, Jim Ellis, Tom Truscott, and Steve Daniel – at Duke University. Usenet has since grown to include thousands of discussion forums, called newsgroups. The messages in these newsgroups are hosted on news servers distributed around the world. New postings made to a particular server migrate to other servers fairly quickly, through a series of server-to-server synchronizing activities. For most of its history, Usenet was accessed using an application very similar to an email client called a newsreader. Now, it has become much more common to access Usenet newsgroups using web-based interfaces like *Google Groups*, which offer far better information management tools.

There is still plenty of evidence of OSS activity in the Usenet space. The GNU project, for example, has its own top-level Usenet category containing many active newsgroups. There are nearly a hundred different Linux-related newsgroups, and a simple search for the phrase "Open Source" at *Google Groups* quickly fetched a half-million postings. However, it would appear that just as the news reader has widely given way to the web browser, OSS stakeholders have been steadily moving over the years to alternative online environments in which to collaborate and converse. Currently, we see the bulk of OSS activity taking place within email mailing lists and on websites.

Nearly every major OSS project is associated with a number of mailing lists that facilitate development, user support, and administration. Perl and Python, for example, each have around 20 high-traffic lists, and the Apache Software Foundation hosts nearly a hundred. The GNU software project probably boasts the most lists – hosting nearly 250 (plus 50 more for the GNOME project)! It should be noted that only a very, very small percentage of these lists are of the announcement/administration variety. The bulk of the lists are highly active environments for collaboration and conversation among developers and users, and in many projects, the main development mailing lists are the primary communication tools used by the core group of developers.

E-mail mailing lists are an interesting medium, which in many ways combine the best qualities of both email and Usenet. For example, email is a one-to-one communication medium (or possibly one to many, using multiple recipients), while Usenet was a many-to-many medium. Mailing lists, which bounce all messages and replies sent to the list out to the entire subscriber base, take after Usenet, and support many-to-many dialogs, the natural mode of discourse in what Raymond famously called the bazaar. Mailing lists also often inherit another important Usenet trait – the possibility of persistence. Many OSS mailing lists maintain web-based archives, which not only ensure the future availability of the information, but also provide convenient tools for searching and manipulating the data. Archived discussions, which represent "self-documentation" of projects, are critical in OSS development. On the other hand, mailing lists take after email in that they are a push medium, rather than a pull medium like Usenet. Newsgroups require the user to actively request information – just as the web does – while mailing lists take the burden off the user by delivering new content without being explicitly requested. Most mailing lists also provide subscribers with the ability to grab a list of other participants (impossible in Usenet), and to request "digest" versions of high-volume lists to reduce information overload.

There is also a tremendous amount of OSS activity on the web itself. First of all, there are the web front-ends for Usenet (as discussed above), and web front-ends for a number of other web-based mailing list archives, which again make conversations persistent and highly searchable. There are also discussion forums that are purely web-based, although we do not see many of the major project coordinators hosting them (they seem to favor mailing lists). At SourceForge, both mailing lists and web-based discussion forums are available to support project collaboration. Activity levels in the two environments vary greatly – we see some projects with thousands of forum postings and only a dozen messages in their mailing list archives, with other projects reversing that trend. Interestingly, there does not appear to be a consistent relationship between CVS activity and discussion forum/mailing list activity, although this deserves further research. For example, we occasionally see projects with very little (public) conversation, but high levels of activity in the CVS repository, suggesting that other modes of collaboration are being used, whether private email, Usenet, or non-computer-mediated modalities.

Although some SourceForge groups make good use of them, purely web-based forums seem to come into their own as a tool for disseminating and reacting to news, opinion, and advice (for example, at Slashdot) rather than as a tool for collaboration. Part of this is due to the "pull" nature of the medium – but it is also likely caused by the lack of privacy and accountability on the web. In a mailing list, users can account for each other – even the lurkers – while on the web, they cannot.

The web also serves as a reference repository that supports community activities. There are an enormous number of web-based periodicals, books, and tutorials related to OSS and OSS technologies – for the most part driven by commerce, not community, but nonetheless an important part of OSS's online environment.

Before we move offline, it's worth taking one last look at CVS (which we discussed in Chapter 6). While Usenet, email, mailing lists, and the web might be the online environment in which decisions are made, CVS remains the most common online environment in which decisions are implemented. As we noted in Chapter 6, CVS is far from the "bleeding edge" of configuration management technology. Nonetheless, it has served well as the configuration management tool of choice for a large percentage of the most well-known and ambitious OSS projects, and is the default tool for the enormous community of developers at SourceForge. CVS is also an important tool for researching and better understanding OSS, for two reasons. First, it provides a history of the projects it serves, and a quantifiable account of activity within the project. Second, the way CVS is used (e.g., who has write privileges) tells a lot about the different leadership structures found in different projects – e.g., the use of CVS in the FreeBSD Project vs. the Apache HTTP Server Project (Fitzgerald and Feller, 2001).

OSS offline

Above, we said that OSS stakeholders primarily interact in virtual environments, using Internet tools. Primarily, but not exclusively; the physical world also plays an important role. In Stallman's (1999a) account of the origin of the FSF, he expresses nostalgia for the *physical* community of people sharing software to which he once belonged, both at the MIT Media Lab, and before. In many ways, that face-to-face community is re-emerging, and although much OSS activity occurs in virtual spaces, there is an increasing amount of "real" world activity as well.

One important, and fairly recent, trend is the increase in the number of co-located OSS development teams. Companies like Red Hat, IBM, and Zelerate (formerly Open Sales) produce Open Source code on a daily basis. While they still leverage the globally distributed developer and user communities that characterize OSS, they are also bringing core developers together in more traditional, physical settings. Likewise, we see evidence of growth among co-located user communities. Online communities (of any kind) tend to be bounded by interest (cf. Hagel and Armstrong, 1997; Rheingold, 1994). Offline communities, on the other hand, are often geographically bounded. Lately we see enormous growth in the network of local Linux User Groups (LUGs), Apache User Groups, etc. – all of which are bounded by geography as well as by interest. In addition to these local groups, major international conferences like O'Reilly's Open Source Convention and the various Apache conferences physically bring together OSS developers and users who might have been interacting in virtual spaces for years.

The physical world does more than provide a venue for online colleagues to occasionally meet face-to-face – it impacts OSS in many ways. Too often, the question "Where is Open Source?" is answered glibly – "in cyberspace," "everywhere and nowhere," etc. Besides being glib, these answers are wrong. The people using and developing OSS products are very much physical beings in a physical world.

For example, Internet-based software distribution makes OSS development possible. However, it can be argued that the widespread desire among users for the physical convenience of a CD-ROM-based installation of an operating system keeps many OSS companies in business! Likewise, OSS is affected by political and physical geography. Saying that OSS is geographically boundless is as accurate as saying that the Internet economy is frictionless (recent experience has shown it most certainly is not). Geographic and political boundaries loom large in OSS, where the functionality of software might be legal in one area of the world and illegal in other areas (for example, strong encryption export regulations, or the arrest of Dmitry Sklyarov for opening Adobe's eBook software).

Finally, although certainly *international*, it is not clear that OSS is really and truly *global*. Studies like those referenced in Chapter 6 would seem to indicate that OSS development remains an activity primarily of the developed world, and more specifically, the Western developed world. This trend is particularly interesting in light of the high hopes placed on OSS as a means to bridge the massive technology gaps within underdeveloped nations (cf. Bokhari and Rehman, 1999). Nevertheless, the OSS community certainly exhibits a strong sense of "global" thinking. The collaborative, mostly gift-based development of Linux and Apache are impressive. Just as impressive are the voluntary efforts supporting the documentation of OSS products, and the subsequent translation of these documents into dozens of languages. Indeed, Scacchi (2001) has recommended the use of the term "open software" as opposed to "open *source* software," as it better reflects all the ancillary activities and the development process, and avoids what could become a myopic focus on just the source code. We see in the wider OSS community a desire both for platform independence and for internationalization – both important aspects of technological excellence, and technological freedom.

The "when?" of OSS

Many of the temporal characteristics of OSS have already been discussed in previous chapters. In this section we take a closer look at the "timing" of OSS events. Specifically, we discuss the rapid evolution of OSS products, the use of synchronous and asynchronous communication and collaboration tools in OSS, and the timing of key events in the OSS development and distribution life cycles.

Rapid evolution

Due to a number of the characteristics of the OSS process discussed in Chapter 6 – like parallel development, prompt feedback, and rapid release schedules – OSS development teams are potentially capable of rapidly developing production-quality code. This fast-forward quality of OSS is interesting, and certainly desirable in a world of missed deadlines, one aspect of the "software crisis." However, it is perhaps more important that OSS product families often have the capacity to change much more quickly than their proprietary counterparts – fixing problems, adding new functionality, or even making significant, innovative leaps. Innovation in the hardware industry has been incredibly rapid – perhaps unprecedented – to the extent that it is enshrined in Moore's Law, namely that hardware processor capability doubles every 18 months or so. Yet software innovation is very slow, measured generally in decades (e.g., the killer app of the 1980s, of the 1990s, etc.) rather than in months (cf. Friedman, 1989). It has been argued that the OSS development process can perhaps address this disparity. Raymond (2001), Fogel (1999), Kuwabara (2000), and Andersen and Valente (1999) are just a few who have argued that the dynamics of the "bazaar" provides the flexibility, variety, and ruthless selection which seeds evolutionary change. The *modus operandi* of OSS certainly encourages adaptation and mutation, an interesting fact in the face of Microsoft's allegations that OSS in fact stifles innovation (CNET Investor, 2001). There is, however, a pronounced need for further research to validate the claims that OSS is capable of more rapid evolution than proprietary software.

Synchronicity/asynchronicity

Earlier in this chapter, we discussed the fact that the majority of OSS collaboration and conversation takes place online. On the one hand, this practice enables OSS software to be developed "in Internet time," fueling the rapidity discussed above. Email, for example, allows for nearly instantaneous communication between developers, a requirement if truly distributed teams are to work at an acceptable pace. On the other hand, we see that the OSS community favors asynchronous modes of communication – email, mailing lists, newsgroups, discussion forums – to synchronous tools like chat, videoconferencing, etc.[1] The question is why? One reason might be in the permanence found in asynchronous tools – OSS thus becomes a self-documenting phenomenon. Another explanation can be found in the quality that comes from considered thought – asynchronous tools allow OSS stakeholders to resolve issues with sufficient time for reflection. Finally, asynchronicity is the mode of choice for truly worldwide communities. Synchronous modes of communication – like the mobile phone – are useful for when a member of an organization needs to act in step with other members while away from the "base camp." OSS doesn't necessarily need this kind of tool. Rather, asynchronous communication technologies like mailing lists allow developers from a variety of time zones to work with a smooth continuity – creating a software development team on which "the sun never sets."

---

[1] Synchronous communication tools like IRC are, of course, in use (see http://www.mozilla.org/community.html for one example). We merely argue that the asynchronous channels are more popular.

Similarly, CVS neatly blends synchronous and asynchronous modes to support the OSS process. On the one hand, CVS, as its name indicates, supports concurrency, and addresses the need to resolve conflicting commitments made simultaneously. On the other hand, CVS allows developers to check out code and thus work on it asynchronously and in parallel with other developers. This suggests that while the implementation of change (the commit) requires tools that operate in real time, the OSS community prefers to make decisions and explore solutions in more leisurely and flexible environments.

Timing

Timing is critical, in OSS as in anything. The first timing-related question we pose is when is a technology ready to be Opened? Every technology goes through phases – stages of maturity, stages of adoption – and it is critical to understand the combination of stages needed to make the OSS model truly viable.[2] Raymond has written several times on the question of at what point in a technology's life is it ready to be Open Source? In an interview with Salon.com (Leonard, 1998) he states:

> I'm not against closed source in absolute principle, I just think it's an inferior, shoddy way to do things most of the time. But I've sat down and thought about under what circumstances it makes sense to be closed vs. open. And I've identified a spectrum with two extremes of software that you might want.

> On the one hand you have research-intensive software. A real good example of that is something everyone is talking about right now – iris scanning for biometrics. It's a research intensive technology that

---

[2] Interestingly, Stallman, known to be unyielding on the topic, asks the reverse question – at what stage does total freedom become irrelevant – when he described why the LGPL might be used only for libraries from which the Free Software community gained no advantages from GPLing.

depends on algorithms nobody else has, and it's only being prototyped in relatively small systems where reliability is not a huge concern. On the other end of the spectrum you have what I call implementational kinds of software. The paramount case of that is something like an office mailing list. All the techniques for running mailing lists are very well known. There is no knowledge in particular, there is no special algorithm — the big problems are robustness, reliability and scalability, and that situation is where the Open Source model really, really shines, because what you want at that point is massive peer review, to get your reliability.

The interesting thing to notice is that individual software technology is always moving from one end to the other of the spectrum. A perfect example is real-time 3-D animation. Five years ago, when [the computer game] "Doom" came out, that was a research-intensive technology. Few people knew how to do it well and you could capture a lot of value by adding a new trade secret – it made sense to be closed. Come 1998 and lots of people know how to do it. There are several alternative packages out there, some of them are free, it's being implemented in larger and larger systems where again your problems are scalability, reliability and robustness, rather than just getting the details of the animation right.

Well, the implication of this is that at some point during the last five years the payoff curves crossed over – there came a point when the gain from peer review exceeded the gain from holding the software captive and having it be a trade secret. The interesting question is where is that crossover point? How do you identify that? My thinking now is that every software technology goes through the same evolution. I am beginning to think that this may be the fundamental software management question of the 21st century: Where is the crossover point? And I love to say these things to business people, because this is exactly the kind of optimization problem that gives them enormous erections. And if I can get them thinking in those terms, we've won.

In *The Magic Cauldron* (Raymond, 2001MC) he argues the point more formally, writing that OSS has the highest payoff for software which requires a high degree of reliability (cf. Neumann 1998, 2000a, 2000b; Nakakoji and Yamamoto, 2001), which requires peer review to verify quality, which is considered a mission-critical business capital good (see the trend towards corporate adoption of OSS discussed in Chapter 7), which establishes or enables a common infrastructure and which relies on algorithms, etc., within the common body of engineering knowledge (see Chapter 5). A related, micro-level question is "when is an individual OSS product ready to be released?" There seem to be many different opinions on the topic. Raymond (2001CatB) has outlined two minimal requirements to be met before software is released into the OSS community: the software must run, and it must convince potential co-developers of its future potential. Others set the standards higher (Nakakoji and Yamamoto, 2001).

Above, we ask the question, when is the right time to begin the OSS process – a related question is when (or if) it ever ends. In Chapter 7 we noted that OSS products outlive their "owners" and Raymond (2001CatB) has stated that the last duty of the developer who tires of his or her project is to find a replacement. But longevity is only one aspect of this question. First of all, we see in the rapid release cycles of OSS a constant alternation between implementation, testing, feedback, and change – what some have called an extreme spiral model and others a beta-release that never ends. On a related note, we see the extension of the development life cycle into the distribution life cycle; indeed the two cycles have become difficult to distinguish (van der Hoek, 2000).

Conclusion

In this chapter we have explored the major online environments in which OSS stakeholders interact, namely mailing lists, newsgroups, and web-based forums. We asserted that the community seems to value the mailing list over all other forms of communication – for its accountability, its many-to-many nature, and its possibility of persistence. We also examined the offline interactions of stakeholders, and argued that the physical world and physical geography continue to heavily impact the OSS community. Finally, we examined the temporal characteristics of OSS, noting the preference of the community for asynchronous communication, and the criteria by which events in the OSS product life cycle are timed.

9

World-view: what are the motivations behind Open Source development?

In this chapter, we discuss the world-view category of our framework. Specifically, we discuss the technological, economic, and socio-political motivations underlying participation in Open Source Software. For each of these three perspectives, we further subdivide the discussion into the micro level of individual developers and the macro level of the broader community.

A framework for classifying OSS motivations

The underlying motivation behind participation in OSS has been the subject of a considerable amount of research (e.g., Hars and Ou, 2001; Lerner and Tirole, 2000; Raymond, 2001). In this chapter, we propose a framework that considers three broad motivational areas (technological, economic, and socio-political), and further subdivides each of these into the micro level (individual developers), and the macro level (organization/community). This framework is illustrated in Table 9.1, where the motivational factors in each of the resulting six categories are summarized. Each category is discussed in detail in the subsequent sections.

TABLE 9.1 Motivations for OSS

	Micro level (individual)	Macro level (organization/community)
Technological motivations	To meet a personal technological need To exploit the efficiency of peer review, etc. To work with "bleeding-edge" technology	To address the software crisis – particularly poor quality To share tedious development tasks (testing, documentation) with users To leverage the OSS community for R&D To promote innovation To ensure transparency of the application
Economic motivations	To gain future career benefits To improve coding skills To "strike it rich" through stock options, etc. Low opportunity cost – nothing to lose	To exploit investor infatuation with OSS To embrace the paradigm shift from software as a commodity industry to consumer-driven service model To raise mind-share and strengthen brand To exploit indirect revenues – selling related products and services, accessorizing, etc. To make software affordable in developing countries To cut costs – cheaper platform than proprietary alternatives

TABLE 9.1 continued

	Micro level (individual)	Macro level (organization/community)
Socio-political motivations	Ego gratification and signaling incentives	Social movements require an enemy – e.g. Microsoft
	Intrinsic motivation of coding	Overcomes "digital divide"
	Sense of belonging to a community	Ideology – software must be free
	Altruism	Model for wider domain – future model for work

Technological micro-level (individual) motivation

At this level, the technical motivation for participating in OSS development revolves around what Raymond called "scratching a personal itch." Almost all of the most widely known and successful OSS projects seem to have been initiated by someone who had a technical need that was not being addressed by available proprietary (or OSS) technology. For example:

- Linus Torvalds needing a version of Unix for his PC to the end result of Linux;

- Eric Allman needing a convenient way of distributing mail to users with several email addresses on different machines at Berkeley to the end result of Sendmail;

- Larry Wall needing a way to generate web pages automatically without the cumbersome overhead of writing C programs to the end result of Perl;

- Don Knuth needing some way of conveniently type-setting documents to the end result of T_eX.

The common denominator in all is that some individual, or small group, needed some kind of specific technical functionality otherwise unavailable.

While personal requirements are a strong technical motivator for starting a project, the advantages of peer review, collaborative development, and other aspects of the OSS process discussed in Chapter 6 are the technical motivators for releasing the software into the OSS space.

There is also another technical motivation for participating in an existing OSS project, namely the opportunity to work with "bleeding-edge" technology. This opportunity is particularly attractive to developers in a traditional development environment who may be faced with using "old" tools and technology, because that is all that is available or is mandated for their particular development project. Additionally, it is generally accepted that MS Windows is a difficult platform to write for. Thus, OSS products can be technically superior, and easier to work with. Torvalds, in a *New York Times* interview (cited in Pfaff and David, 1998), probably captures the spirit of this technological rather than economic motivation for OSS best:

> You use a Windows machine and the golden rule is 'Save and save often'. It's scary how people have grown used to the idea that computers are unreliable when it is not the computer at all – it's the operating system that just doesn't cut it.

Technological macro-level (organization/community) motivation

At the macro level, one of the principal motivations of OSS is that it directly addresses the software crisis. Whether or not one accepts the extent to which such a crisis exists, it is certainly the case that the conventional means of production for software is problematic. Software typically takes too long to develop, costs too much, and doesn't work very well when it is delivered – all three aspects appear to be directly addressed by OSS.

Firstly, the time-scale for development is dramatically altered in OSS. All OSS projects exhibit rapid evolution, as discussed in previous chapters. Likewise, given that much, although by no means all, OSS development comprises voluntary contributions, the cost aspect of software crisis appears to be addressed. It is important that this be qualified, however, since the true cost of OSS development has never been estimated. It may often consist of highly paid developers doing work on the sly during company time and being paid on the assumption that they are working solely on *bona fide* traditional projects for the organization. (If OSS were to scale up to become a mass phenomenon, this masking of its true cost would be clearly problematic.) Finally, the quality aspect of the software crisis is undoubtedly addressed in OSS, as OSS products are generally chosen by the technically savvy who will not be dissuaded by FUD tactics, nor are they likely to be persuaded by a slick marketing campaign. No OSS product will require any *Start Me Up* marketing campaign, which may be bad news for the Rolling Stones. Independent peer review by a large and talented pool of developers is likely to lead to high quality software, and these are central aspects of the OSS development process.

> FUD is an acronym for Fear, Uncertainty, Doubt, and it represents a "dirty tricks" strategy which has been used particularly in the computer industry to help undermine competitors (see Irwin, 1998 for an interesting discussion of some examples).

> It is reliably reported that the *Rolling Stones* received a $100m payment from Microsoft for the rights to use the *Start Me Up* song to advertise Windows 95 worldwide.

There are interesting parallels between software development and the evolution of the automobile and telephone. In both the latter cases, it was assumed that the extent to which they would achieve widespread use would be fundamentally limited by the need for the intervention of a skilled expert in all instances of use. Thus, it was assumed that all telephone calls would require the intervention of a telephone operator. Similarly, it was assumed that all automobile journeys would require the skills of a specialized chauffeur. These bottlenecks were expected to limit the use of these technologies. The situation is somewhat analogous in the software industry, where although it is pervasive, the shortage of skilled personnel is a serious constraint. However, in theory at any rate, OSS can address this. Tasks such as testing, documentation, and requirements elaboration, which are tedious and occupy so much development time in the traditional software development model, can actually be delegated to the user community in the OSS model. Indeed, some examples of such a usage mode for OSS have been reported (see Aoki *et al.*, 2001 and Schmidt and Porter, 2001). In these initiatives, code contributions are not actively sought; rather the user community is often solicited to complete other, more tedious tasks.

Also, in keeping with an overall skills shortage, some organizations are leveraging OSS to perform some of the R&D function. The most obvious example of this is probably Mozilla, whereby Netscape released the source of their Communicator browser, and were permitted to use a license that allows them to incorporate any useful functionality into their proprietary products. There are several other similar scenarios. Apple have released Darwin, the core of the MacOSX server system, under an Open Source license, and can thus take advantage of any extra functionality that may be added.

There are a number of other technical motivations for organizational participation in, or adoption of, OSS products and processes. IBM, whose involvement in OSS is discussed in Chapter 7, has embraced OSS for a number of reasons, but a significant one is said to be the innovation that the OSS process affords. The cross-pollination of ideas is expected to facilitate discovery. Hewlett-Packard, frequently to the forefront in knowledge-intensive initiatives, have also committed strongly to the OSS initiative, both in the SourceXchange project and also in their initiation of an OSS model to facilitate sharing of knowledge within HP, termed "Corporate Source" (see Dinkelacker and Garg, 2001). Also, other very wealthy organizations, such as NASA and the National Security Agency (NSA), have adopted OSS products for technical reasons. In the case of NASA, the total transparency afforded by access to the source code is a primary reason for choosing to use the Linux operating system. It can be tested exhaustively, and the security of their operations is not dependent on any "black-box" system. Similarly, the NSA has created a special version of the Linux kernel to incorporate security features deemed necessary in their environment.

While many organizations might be shocked at the extent to which their key infrastructure is dependent on OSS products with no legal owner or contracted service support agreement, Raymond has controversially suggested that:

> it will probably not be long before buying closed-source software for
> your key infrastructure is considered the height of irresponsibility.

Economic micro-level (individual) motivation

While it appeared initially that there were no economic incentives behind developer participation in OSS, more sophisticated economic analyses have overturned this naïve assumption (e.g., Hars and Ou, 2001 and Lerner and Tirole, 2000).

Lerner and Tirole (2000) ground their discussion of the motivations of individual developers in the economics of *signaling incentives*. The latter is an umbrella term capturing both *ego gratification* and *career concern* incentives. The *ego gratification* incentive is based on peer recognition, and is discussed later in the socio-political motivations section of this chapter. The *career concern* incentive relates to the fact that working on an OSS project may enhance future job prospects for developers – after all, Linus Torvalds states that his reward for working on Linux has been that he will never have any difficulty in getting a job – his resumé, as he puts it, contains just one word: Linux. Likewise, developers who may feel mired in stolid old-fashioned technology in their everyday work can improve their skill base by participating in projects using the latest technologies on OSS projects, thus allowing them to configure their CV to be more attractive to prospective employers. This obviously applies to students as well, as they get the opportunity to participate in real projects. Also, it is well known that employers scan the credit lists of OSS products to identify promising talent. Thus, it is a good way to advertise one's development skills.

Many OSS developers have admitted that they put more effort into their coding in the first place because they knew that respected peers would be inspecting their efforts. Even Linus Torvalds admits that he was concerned that Linux would be good enough to avoid shameful embarrassment before he considered making the initial version available for public feedback in 1991 (Torvalds and Diamond, 2001). However, he wanted feedback, and all developers improve their coding skills through feedback. Strong evidence of such a motivation in practice may be gleaned from a survey of OSS developers involved in a range of OSS projects, conducted by Hars and Ou (2001). They found that over 70 percent of respondents reported the desire to improve their programming skills as being their motivation to contribute to OSS.

Also, there is direct evidence of an economic motivation, as it has emerged that much OSS development is actually being paid for. The examples of IBM, Hewlett-Packard, Netscape, Cosource, and SourceXchange have indicated that there is a demand for OSS developers who can be paid for their work. Also, in a survey of the FreeBSD project, Jorgensen (2001) found that 41 percent of developers were paid by their employer for the development they undertook on the project. Similarly, in their survey, Hars and Ou (2001) found that 50 percent of respondents were paid for their OSS work.

Another facet of the career concern incentive might be that those participating in OSS projects may get offered shares in commercial companies – given the phenomenal performance of OSS-related IPOs, this is indeed significant. Eric Raymond is estimated to have become wealthy to the tune of $47m when VA Linux went public in 1999,[1] while Linus Torvalds estimated that he was worth $20m (Torvalds and Diamond, 2001). Yet, Torvalds' lack of desire to make money on Linux in the early days is legendary. Indeed, when individuals around the globe offered to send him money for Linux, he requested postcards instead. Also, the loan on his 386 PC on which he developed Linux was eventually paid off from the proceeds

---

[1] Raymond's VA Linux wealth is on paper only, he has never sold any stock nor has he ever requested payment for his advocacy work.

of a collection from Linux hackers. He attributes this lack of interest in money to having been

> brought up under the influence of a diehard academic grandfather and a diehard communist father.
>
> (TORVALDS AND DIAMOND, 2001, P.94).

However, the stock options which he accepted from various Linux ventures paid off for him, in a manner which he never really expected, and certainly helped him fulfil one of his central goals in life, that of having fun. Yet, he is extremely careful not to endanger his reputation as someone who can be trusted with evolving Linux, so much so that he admits to refusing a $10m offer to become a board member in a fledgling Linux company.

However, as not all OSS developers can aspire to such fortune-making, and the resentment that this might engender could be critically harmful, there may be scope for remuneration for OSS work with more innovative payment mechanisms. Certainly, a micro-payment system for small amounts of work has not been feasible or practical in the workplace up to now, but this may be feasible in the world of e-commerce today. Several writers have discussed the lessons that the OSS model may provide for the future of work, and have speculated on how reward schemes could be implemented to cater for this (Dinkelacker and Garg, 2001; Masum, 2001), including micro-payments, the "Street Performer Protocol," and completion bonds.

Finally, in an economic sense, developers may have nothing to gain in economic terms by keeping developments to themselves. Thus, in a game-theoretic sense, there is nothing to lose by opting for OSS, even if any financial benefits do not seem immediately obvious.

Economic macro-level (organization/community) motivation

Initially, the idea that OSS could be economically viable for commercial organizations seemed the most problematic aspect of the whole phenomenon. Yet, even if the notion of making money from OSS might not sit comfortably with all, there are undoubtedly several business models which suggest how OSS can be used to make money (Markus *et al.*, 2000; Raymond, 2001MC). As the Mozilla project leader, Jamie Zawinksi, put it:

> Netscape didn't get into the Open Source business because they were being nice. They did it because it made business sense.

Certainly, there is much evidence that the revenue-generating capacity of OSS is not as outrageous as it may initially have seemed. The staggering performance of Red Hat and VA Linux in their initial IPO launches in 1999 suggests that there may be vast amounts of money in OSS, although this has to be tempered somewhat by the prevailing dot.com madness at the time. More importantly, beginning with the first quarter of fiscal year 2002 (ended May 31, 2001), Red Hat is a legitimate, in the black, profit-earning company.

A persuasive argument that has been advanced is that the software industry may be undergoing a paradigm shift from a commodity-based model to one based on customer service. Ironically, the paradigm shift to the software-as-a-commodity model was initiated in the main by Microsoft who wrested control of the industry from the primarily hardware-oriented model dominated by IBM and other major hardware vendors. Recognizing that a march has been stolen on them by the OSS community, Microsoft have repositioned themselves with a number of initiatives, including making the source code of some of their products available to leading customers, as described earlier. However, of more significance is the company's .Net strategy whereby corporations will lease software from Microsoft instead of buying it outright. Describing the strategy, Robert McDowell, vice president for worldwide services at Microsoft, suggested (Smyth, 2001):

> It's a brand, our attempt to put an umbrella around everything we are doing and the products we are building. It will enable us to offer software as a service.

The new shift from a commodity product model to one based on customer service makes much sense from an economic point of view. Software has zero reproduction costs, but has very high service and maintenance costs. Yet, it is a well-established fact that the vast proportion of the total cost of software development is incurred in the maintenance phase – with reliable estimates varying from 70 percent (Boehm, 1976) to 80 percent (Flaatten *et al.*, 1989).

This suggests that the model for proprietary software, based on the manufacturing model of a high purchase price with a low maintenance fee, does not reflect the reality of the cost distribution in practice. This is recognized in the OSS model where the software is distributed for a nominal fee and companies then compete on service to the consumer. (Ironically, by adopting a high service fee model, OSS distributors can exploit the unquestionably high reliability of OSS products in that support costs are much less than for traditional software development.) Brand management becomes critical and customers learn to value a brand they can trust in terms of quality, reliability, and consistency. In these business conditions, OSS companies can learn from the experiences of companies such as Perrier, Ballygowan, and Heinz, where brand image has been successfully exploited in a highly competitive consumer-driven market. Brand importance is certainly evident in the quote from Microsoft's McDowell above.

In light of this, the opportunity of OSS to raise a product's profile among potential consumers is significant. Raymond (1999) reports the example of Digital Creations who had developed a useful object publishing package, Zope,[2] and were looking for funding. Their venture capitalist advised them to place the product in Open Source, advice that appeared at first to be very controversial as it was releasing the "crown jewels" of the source code intellectual property. However, the counter-argument was that OSS would raise the profile of Zope considerably. Also, R&D costs would be lower as much development could take place in the OSS community for free.

---

[2] Zope Object Publishing Environment – yet another recursive acronym.

Ironically, Zope has chosen not to bear the actual OSI Certification mark, as previously discussed.

Raymond (2001) presents a number of economic models that apply to the indirect sale value of OSS. One of the interesting models refers to the accessorizing of OSS, although probably not in the conventional form of T-shirts and mugs.[3] This appears to have been a factor in OSS in that one of the people who has benefited most from OSS has been the publisher Tim O'Reilly whose company has published the books that have sold in such vast quantities.

The shift to a consumer-driven market highlights the other end of the OSS economic model in that it appears to represent a win-win model. In "developing" countries, software costs that may appear quite trivial are often prohibitively expensive. If the average annual salary is $100, then $150 for a Microsoft Windows license puts it out of reach. Thus, OSS has become a godsend for these countries. Many organizations in the developing world also need to cut costs, and the cost of supporting 1,000 users on a Linux platform is much less than the cost of using a Microsoft or Sun platform (DiBona et al., 1999; Yee, 1999).

While the OSS model appears to represent a paradigm shift in the software industry (discussed in Chapter 10), Young (1999) identifies other industries where similar principles apply. In the legal industry, for example, one cannot patent legal arguments for exclusive use; rather, all are free to make use of previous judgments and precedents. In the automobile industry, parts from the same suppliers are assembled into various brand-named cars. Assembly and service are core aspects of the business. Although Young does not extend the analogy to academe, certain similarities, particularly on the supply side, are striking. For example, it is the case that peer review and reputation are critical in academe; also, there is a tendency to recruit the most competent "stars." These are both important aspects of the OSS culture also.

---

[3] Actually, Think Geek does just that.

Socio-political micro-level (individual) motivation

There are several motivational factors for OSS that can be classified in this category, including ego gratification, intrinsic motivation, the sense of community, and altruism.

Ego gratification is one of the signaling incentives developed by Lerner and Tirole (2000) as a way of explaining the motivation of individual developers contributing to OSS. Developers working on traditional development projects may face long delays in getting feedback on their work. After all, the average project development life cycle has been estimated to be 18 months (Flaatten *et al.*, 1989), and durations of up to five years are not unknown (Taylor and Standish, 1982). Thus, developers experience a significant "rush" from seeing their code in use more quickly in OSS projects. Also, the recognition they do receive is often from peers they truly respect, rather than from managers and users within their own organization, whom they may not respect to the same extent. Bergquist and Ljungberg (2001) discuss the OSS developer motivational issue also in some detail and they refer to the phenomenon as obeying an *attention economy*, in that the more attention an OSS developer can attract, the greater the enhancement of status that is achieved.

Hars and Ou (2001) discuss the *intrinsic motivation* factor. This is complemented by the seminal work by Maslow (1970) in the area of motivation that identifies the self-actualization and esteem needs of individuals. Viewed through this lens, working on OSS is seen as akin to pursuing a hobby that is intrinsically satisfying. Hars and Ou exemplify this with a quote from an OSS developer who explained his work on OSS as fulfilling an "innate desire to code, and code, and code until the day I die."

This is further evidenced by a Linux contributor, Ali Abdin, who posted a message on the news group describing his feelings, with shades of Leonardo diCaprio in *Titanic*, after successfully contributing to Linux development:

An array of processors running Linux achieved the rendering for the special effects in the *Titanic* movie. At the time, it was the most expensive movie ever made, so presumably, the choice of Linux was for performance rather than monetary reasons.

I felt on top of the world, that I can program anything … I felt as a mother would feel giving birth to a child, giving it life, for the first time.

However, the intrinsic satisfaction is captured best by Torvalds who cites the importance of having fun as one of his primary goals in life, and Linux development represented a significant opportunity for him to have fun. This was far more important to him than sharing code. As he describes it:

I remember Lars Wirzenius,[4] around the time I was writing Linux, decided to buy XENIX, SCO's version of Unix, and i think I remember he tried to make excuses, like, 'Don't take this the wrong way.' I personally don't think I ever cared. He eventually switched, but it wasn't a big deal for me. To me the fact that people used it was nice, and it was wonderful that I got comments back, but at the same time it was not that important. I didn't want to spread the gospel. I was proud of having people use my code, but I don't remember ever having the feeling that I wanted to share that with anybody. And I didn't think it was the most important thing on Earth. And I didn't think that I was doing something really important because a hundred people were using my software. It was more like it was fun. And that's how I feel about it today.

(TORVALDS AND DIAMOND, 2001, PP. 108–9)

The sense of belonging to a community also appears to be a central motivator for OSS developers. While individual developers might feel powerless against the might of the opposition, belonging to a global community engenders a feeling of power in the leveling of the playing-field. The esoteric and often undocumented norms and taboos discussed in Chapter 6 are indicative of the community nature of OSS. Thus, the sense of humor, use of recursive acronyms,

---

[4] A close personal friend of Torvalds who organized the official launch of Linux at the University of Helsinki.

and the use of esoteric names and labels from science fiction are all part of this culture, and outsiders do not gain access easily. Himanen (2001) relates the amusing case of FBI agents who were investigating the theft of source code by a cracker group, Nu Prometheus, but who were referred to as New Prosthesis by the FBI agents.

Raymond (2001RotH) exemplifies the "us vs. them" community aspect of OSS very well:

> My tribe is waging a struggle to raise the quality and reliability expectations of software consumers and overturn the standard operating procedures of the software industry. We face entrenched opposition with a lot of money and mind-share and monopoly power. It's not an easy fight, but the logic and economics is clear; we can win and we will win. *If*, that is, we stay focused on that goal.

In the Hars and Ou (2001) survey, more than half (52 percent) of respondents cited the sense of community belonging as the reason for their participation in OSS projects. Perhaps, the definitive words on this come from Torvalds (1998):

> … the act of making Linux freely available wasn't some agonizing decision that I took from thinking long and hard on it: it was a natural decision within the community that I felt I wanted to be a part of.

The final motivational factor that applies to OSS developers is that of altruism. This is somewhat related to community in the sense that individual developers will feel the need to help their community. However, it is also related to Maslow's needs in that altruism can be very satisfying and fulfills certain individual needs. Raymond (2001HtN) devotes a lot of attention to this and considers it to be gift giving in a climate of abundance, a variation of the potlatch economy of Indian tribes. Bergquist and Ljungberg draw on Mauss's (1950) work on gift economies to elaborate this rationale in detail (see also Ljungberg, 2000).

Socio-political macro-level (organization/community) motivation

The OSS movement is often portrayed as a communistic collectivist approach; Bob Young, the founder of Red Hat, has adapted the communist manifesto to characterize it as "from the programmers according to their skills, to the users according to their needs" (Young, 1999). Also, Linux has been described as an "impossible public good" (Smith and Kollock, 1999). It is said that all social movements require an enemy, and Microsoft seems to have assumed the mantle of anti-hero for the OSS community. It is common in the parlance of OSS to see references to "Micro$oft," and its employees are labeled "microserfs," thereby serving the purpose of suggesting they occupy a petty place in a dictatorial, "riches *uber alles*" regime. The leaked Halloween Documents (1998) do much to reinforce this stereotype, and Raymond's rhetoric of a tribe engaged in a struggle, mentioned in the previous section, also contributes to this mentality. Ideology thus plays a big part in OSS, be it at the level of not wishing to use any Microsoft products or any other proprietary software. Ironically, Torvalds in describing his first public speaking appearance in 1993 after Linux became a popular phenomenon, unashamedly admits to

> It is not all one-way traffic however. It is reputed that Torvalds' face is emblazoned on dartboards in Microsoft, to which his response has been, "how could anybody possibly miss my nose?"

clinging to my PowerPoint slides (thank God for Microsoft) like a life preserver.

(TORVALDS AND DIAMOND, 2001, P. 114)

Ideology also plays a major part at the level of desiring to rectify global inequities and disparities by providing information technology free to the "developing" countries. This latter, the "digital divide" has been the subject of much discussion. But in a sobering reflection on the issue, Bill Gates, who is doing more than anyone else with his $21bn foundation, has argued that spanning the digital divide was not the most pressing concern for these countries; rather, medicines and vaccines were a far higher priority (*New York Times,* November 3, 2000).

> While the contention that more than 40,000 developers have contributed to Linux development may be dubious, a far more chilling estimate is that more than 40,000 hapless human beings die each day from preventable diseases.

As already mentioned in Chapter 2, ideology has frequently played a part in the history of free software and OSS, from BSD, through the Free Software Foundation, right on to Open Source Software. The BSD distribution was not made available in South Africa during the apartheid regime, for example. Also, Stallman's FSF was premised on the fundamental belief that all software source should be available to anyone who wanted it. The FSF tried to provide a complete family of free software alternatives to commercial packages, and many were drawn by such an ideology, even if Open Source emerged as a means of diluting the blatant ideological connotations of free software.

It should be noted, however, that OSS is not a movement that can be pinned down easily as one that follows a particular ideology. Linus Torvalds is quite negative about an undue emphasis on idealism, suggesting that in his experience, "idealistic people are boring and sometimes scary" (Torvalds and Diamond, 2001, p. 165), and that he himself has never been "the selfless, ego-free, techno-lovechild of the hallucinating press" (*ibid.*, p. 118).

More recent accounts of OSS have stressed the potential of transferring the model beyond software to the organization of work itself – an issue discussed again in Chapter 10 (Cook, 2001; Dinkelacker and Garg, 2001; Markus *et al.*, 2000; O'Reilly, 2000). Tim O'Reilly has talked about OSS being the natural language of the networked society. In the research world, a significant boost for the OSS model arose from Dr Harold Varmus, director of the prestigious and influential National Institutes of Health, who pledged to bypass conventional peer-reviewed academic channels and publish the Directorate's research immediately on their website, thereby making it more readily available in a more timely fashion to anyone who might wish to benefit (Blume, 1999).

Cook (2001) speculates on the transfer of OSS practices to traditional software development, arguing that it could lead to increased outsourcing as development tasks could be distributed worldwide over the Internet, thereby creating a larger virtual organization of developers. Dinkelacker and Garg (2001) describe an initiative within Hewlett-Packard, labeled "Corporate Source." The intention is to leverage the huge pool of employee knowledge within HP, and is an attempt at realizing the observation of HP CEO Lew Platt that "if HP knew what HP knows, we would be three times as profitable." The intention of the Corporate Source initiative is to leverage employee skills within the company – HP employ over 30,000 engineers – without compromising the intellectual property issue that would arise if the information was to be disseminated outside the company.

Appropriately, we leave the last word on this to Raymond (2001RotH) who, as a self-proclaimed "theorist and ambassador for Open Source," is in no doubt that OSS has a future beyond software, but cautions against moving too quickly:

> I expect the open-source movement to have essentially won its point about software within three to five years. Once that is accomplished, and the results have been manifest for a while, they will become part of the background culture of non-programmers. At *that* point it will become more appropriate to try to leverage open-source insights in wider domains. In the meantime, even if we hackers are not making an ideological noise about it, we will still be changing the world.

10

Critical questions and future research

Having analyzed the various aspects of Open Source Software – qualification, transformation, stakeholders, environment, and world-view – we now turn to a more informal discussion of the many paradoxes and tensions which continue to surround this phenomenon, and recommend directions for future research. Despite the growth in OSS research, some influential commentators have argued that the phenomenon has not yet been captured definitively (Bollier, 1999; McConnell, 1999).

Preparing for the future

As previously discussed, while OSS has become more popular, it remains controversial. On the one hand we see advocates who suggest that OSS represents a paradigm shift that can finally solve the software crisis. *The Economist*[1] magazine cites research by Forrester that predicts that OSS will directly cause software costs to decrease some 20 percent by 2004. Some proponents suggest the lessons of OSS can be transferred to software development in general (e.g., Cook, 2001; Hissam and Weinstock, 2001), and some go further, identifying OSS as a model that transfers well beyond software development into other industry spheres, for example, economics,

---

[1] April 12, 2001.

governance, law, education, medicine (Bollier, 1999; Dinkelacker and Garg, 2001; Gallivan, 2001; Himanen, 2001; Markus *et al.*, 2000; O'Reilly, 2000; Thompson, 2000), and even the stock market (Schmerken, 2000). Bollier (1999) captures the unbounded ambition of these predictions:

> Open code software could evolve into a powerful new platform for the reinvigoration of the non-commercial civic sector in American society … [it] represents a community and knowledge-building infrastructure without precedent … arguably one of the most powerful potential forms of user empowerments in electronic media.

In the writings of some of the more extreme proponents, OSS often gets ascribed with every boy-scout virtue known to man. An influential commentator, Bob Glass (1999), describes his reaction after reading a glowing account of the promise of OSS:

> I felt I was deep in a wonderland of superlatives and social (rather than software) engineering by the time I finished reading.

However, countering these extreme positive views, there are those who suggest that OSS is just the latest silver bullet in the software industry, that it is over-hyped, a strategy employed by the weak with marginal products to compete with the strong. Certainly, there have been high-profile cases of OSS initiatives which have not been successful (e.g., SourceXchange, Eazel). Also, SuSE, the Linux distributor, has laid off two-thirds of its workforce, as the impact of OSS was found to have been exaggerated. In a similar fashion, VA Linux recently announced plans to lay off 25 percent of its workforce. At the extreme, some influential commentators, such as Bob Metcalfe, inventor of Ethernet and founder of 3Com, have described OSS as "utopian balderdash" (Metcalfe, 1999), and it has even been suggested that OSS is "a disaster waiting to happen" (Sessions, 1999). Indeed, Glass (2000) has dismissed OSS as

> an interesting chapter in software's history, but hardly a ground-rules-

changing one. Anyone who suggests otherwise is at least somewhat delusional about human nature.

Taking the specific case of the Linux operating system, without doubt the most high-profile OSS example, the original creators of the Unix operating system differ in their opinions, with Dennis Ritchie describing Linux as "commendable," while Ken Thompson (1999) positions himself very firmly in the negative camp:

> I view Linux as something that's not Microsoft – a backlash against Microsoft, no more and no less. I don't think it will be very successful in the long run. I've looked at the source and there are pieces that are good and pieces that are not. A whole bunch of random people have contributed to this source, and the quality varies drastically.
>
> My experience and some of my friends' experience is that Linux is quite unreliable. Microsoft is really unreliable but Linux is worse. In a non-PC environment, it just won't hold up.
>
> If you're using it on a single box, that's one thing. But if you want to use Linux in firewalls, gateways, embedded systems, and so on, it has a long way to go.

The last several chapters have left us with two key questions, "Is OSS truly successful?" and, if so, "Is that success sustainable and transferable?" To address these questions, we feel that a considerable amount of further research is required.

Qualification revisited

Chapter 5, Qualification, began an investigation of the definition and characteristic features of OSS. Both of these issues require further research and discussion.

The definition of OSS remains problematic, for two reasons. Firstly, we are witnessing increasingly complex activity in the OSS commercial space, with hybrid business models emerging, and pseudo-OSS processes being adopted (like MS Shared Source and HP

Corporate Source). The OSD is a powerful specification, and quite ably filters out things like shareware and trial software. However, if we are to future-proof our understanding of OSS, we need a larger framework in which to make sense of these changes. Secondly, as we previously noted, the OSS label is still contested by many in the community who see it as a distraction from the philosophical values which they believe made OSS possible in the first place. This contestation has led to infighting and to distracting and discouraging "shifts of allegiance" (e.g., Bruce Perens leaving the OSI). More to the point, the Free Software vs. Open Source label war in some ways crystallizes the disparity in rewards being received by different groups of stakeholders.

The characterization of OSS also requires more research. We do not yet have a solid understanding of the patterns, algorithms, and architectures used in OSS systems. If the OSS process is to be replicated in other software contexts, it is critical that we identify the relationships that exist between the structural characteristics of OSS products and the dynamics of the OSS process. Likewise, if the growing popularity of OSS is to continue, we must empirically validate the claim that OSS products are of high quality, and also identify areas in need of further improvement. One study (Stamelos *et al.*, 2002) addressed this issue of quality in relation to the SuSE Linux 6.0 release. Using the Logiscope code analysis tool, over 600 KLOC (thousand lines of codes) across 100 modules in the SuSE release were examined. The results were as follows:

- 50 percent of components acceptable as is;

- 31 percent required comments;

- 9 percent required further inspection;

- 4 percent required further testing;

- 6 percent would have to be completely rewritten.

These results are really quite average – only half the modules actually meet the standard generally expected in the software industry. However, given the extremely rigorous nature of software selection in the corporate space, and the fact that in spite of switching costs, there is a very high level of OSS adoption in that space, it is unlikely that these results can be taken at face value. Nonetheless, further inquiry is required.

Cathedrals in the bazaar

In Chapter 6 we explored the mechanics of the OSS development process. Again, further research is required. Only a few detailed case studies of actual OSS projects exist (e.g., Raymond, 2001CatB; Mockus *et al.*, 2000; Hamerly *et al.*, 1999), which leaves us with only a tentative generic model of the process.

One of the most pressing questions *vis-à-vis* the OSS process is the accuracy of the "bazaar" metaphor. The conventional wisdom of software engineering suggests that given the inherent complexity of software (Brooks, 1987), it should be developed using tightly coordinated, centralized teams, following a rigorous development process (Paulk *et al.*, 1993). Given that within the software family, the most complex product is arguably that of an operating system, it is reasonable to assume that such a product would require a development process congruent with these

> The IBM OS360 operating system, the focus of Brooks' classic book *The Mythical Man Month*, has been reckoned to be the most complex thing that mankind had ever created.

fundamental software engineering principles. As previously discussed, Raymond (2001CatB) categorizes this mode of development as *cathedral*-style, and contrasts this with *bazaar*-style development, which he felt better characterized the OSS development approach.

The bazaar metaphor was chosen to reflect the babbling, apparent confusion of a middle-Eastern marketplace. The generic OSS software process, which we argued consists of parallel development, distributed and loosely coordinated teams, high levels of communication and negotiation between stakeholders, evolutionary contest between solutions, extreme speed, etc., would appear, at first glance, to be very bazaar-like. However, we would raise the question, is contemporary OSS really a bazaar?

As we argued earlier, there is no single OSS development process. There are many projects – application development in the Linux space (Dempsey *et al.*, 1999), for example – that fit into the bazaar mode quite well. On the other hand, many of the major OSS projects – the XML Apache Project, the Linux kernel, GNOME, FreeBSD, to name but a few – are rigorously structured, and in many ways resemble cathedrals instead (cf. Nakakoji and Yamamoto, 2001; Williams, 2000). Raymond (2001MC), for example, identifies the significant bureaucratic overhead associated with the BSD projects, where, after the patch has been "cleaned up," a Change Log entry must be written and the copyright assignment to the Free Software Foundation (for relevant software components) completed. Development of the Linux kernel is likewise highly structured with modifications being coordinated almost entirely through Torvalds and his "lieutenants."

Whether OSS is a bazaar, a cathedral, or both, the fact remains that deeper documentation of the day-to-day, step-by-step development process is needed. For example, the accuracy of Linus's Law needs to be investigated – is it a matter of enough eyeballs, or the right eyeballs? It seems possible that a sort of inverse Pareto principle is at work in that 80 percent of the bugs may be spotted by 99 percent of the OSS developers, whereas the more difficult 20 percent of the bugs are probably only capable of being identified by about 1 percent of the developers. Likewise, the OSS community has demonstrated a certain lack of interest in formal analysis and design tools, possibly indicating a lack of interest in formal analysis and design itself. While unlikely, this and other aspects of the OSS process require further investigation.

Collectivist vs. individual focus

In Chapters 7 and 9 we discussed the stakeholders participating in OSS and their motivations for doing so. Central to this discussion (and at this point unresolved) is the question of whether OSS is primarily to be understood as a collectivist or individual-focused phenomenon, or both.

The OSS movement is often portrayed as highly community-centered. Bob Young, the founder of Red Hat, has even paraphrased the communist manifesto to characterize it as "from the programmers according to their skills, to the users according to their needs" (Young, 1999). Also, Linux has been described as an "impossible public good" (Smith and Kollock, 1999). Certainly, the massive parallel development and the devotion of time by skilled programmers without a direct monetary incentive seems to support such a collectivist view. When Linux won an award as product of the year from *InfoWorld*, the editors at *InfoWorld* complained that they were unsure as to whom the award should be presented, as there was no legal owner for Linux (Leibovitch, 1999).

Another factor in keeping with the collectivist notion is that there seems to be a requirement for modesty and self-deprecation on the part of originators of OSS projects. This is necessary, as they have to convince others to volunteer their efforts in the belief that their input is required. That is, if a developer initiating an OSS project conveys the impression that the originators are on top of things and no help is needed, then the project will not get off the ground as an OSS project. In this vein, Torvalds openly sought help with Linux from the outset.

Likewise, the suggestion that all contributions are valued reinforces the appearance of collectivism. Rather than just accepting strong technical coding contributions, the argument is that those who cannot write code can write documentation, fulfill the role of testers, or elaborate requirements. Thus, the traditional hierarchy in IS departments whereby the program coding activity is perceived as "superior" to the testing and documentation activities is countered in the OSS approach, thus ensuring that these vitally important activities are not undervalued. Also contributing to the collectivist, public good perception of Open Source software is the fact that it is of huge importance in "developing" countries, who cannot afford to pay the high prices demanded by the vendors of proprietary software. Again, this ties in with the media portrayal of OSS as a David vs. Goliath phenomenon, where the poor struggle with the fabulously rich.

There have been efforts to use the strong flavor of collectivism of OSS as a means of undermining it. A senior Microsoft executive, Jim Allchin (cited in the CNET Investor, 2001), puts the case as follows:

> I'm an American, I believe in the American Way. I worry if the government encourages Open Source, and I don't think we've done enough education of policy makers to understand the threat.

Even if the claim is completely and utterly false, the strength of "the American way" style rhetoric should not be underestimated. Figure 10.1 indicates the manner in which another disruptive technology, Napster, has been portrayed in the US.

In contrast to the evidence above, there are also indications that OSS is a highly individualist phenomenon. The closeness between the names Linux and Linus, for example, betrays an individualistic orientation.[2] It is certainly unlikely that Microsoft would choose to market Windows 2002 as Billux, for example. Furthermore, if one were to pose the question "who are Transmeta?" to an audience with some familiarity with OSS, it is quite likely that the answer would be "they are the company that Linus Torvalds works for." However, if pressed on what Transmeta actually do,[3] the answers would in all probability be less forthcoming.

Further evidence of individualist orientation is the undeniable fact that the OSS culture is fundamentally a reputation-based one, and is persuasively underpinned by the economics of *signaling incentives* on the part of individual developers (Lerner and Tirole, 2000). The

---

[2] To be fair to Linus Torvalds, his first inclination was to name the operating system, freax – a combination of "free," "freak," and an -x ending. However, he was persuaded by Ari Lemke to use the name Linux, which was actually his own private name for the system.

[3] Ironically, one of the founders of Transmeta in 1995 was one Paul Allen, who also co-founded another "successful" startup some years earlier, Microsoft. In another irony, given Torvalds' links to Open Source, Transmeta is a notoriously secretive company – a cause of much concern for Linux devotees at the time. Based in Santa Clara, California, it develops platform solutions for the Mobile Internet Computing market. Transmeta's premier product line is the Crusoe processor for a new class of ultra-light mobile computers.

signaling incentive concept was discussed in Chapter 9, and reiterating briefly here, the term is an umbrella one capturing both *ego gratification* and *career concern* incentives. The *ego gratification*

FIGURE 10.1 (with thanks to Anna Maria Sczepanska)

incentive operates on the basis of peer recognition. Developers working on traditional development projects may face long delays in getting feedback on their work. After all, as already mentioned, software development life cycles can last several years. Thus, developers experience a significant "rush" from seeing their code in use more quickly in OSS projects. Also, the recognition they do receive is often from peers they truly respect, rather than from managers and users within their own organization. Bergquist and Ljungberg (2001) discuss the OSS developer motivational issue also in some detail and they refer to the phenomenon as obeying an *attention economy*, in that the more attention an OSS developer can attract, the greater the enhancement of status that is achieved. Thus, in this context, OSS development may be more akin to Ego*ist* Programming as opposed to Egoless Programming, the term coined by Weinberg (1971).

Certainly, the individualistic territorial nature of OSS is revealed tellingly in some of the flame-wars that have erupted between the leading lights of the movement. Torvalds himself documents the "flamefesting" between himself and Andrew Tanenbaum, the creator of Minix (see Chapter 2) (Torvalds and Diamond, 2001, pp. 98–106). Also, the acrimonious dispute between OSS founders, Raymond and Perens, has been well documented, and is discussed in the next section. However, even at the level of the ordinary OSS developer "foot soldiers," acrimonious squabbles can be found which bear all the hallmarks of the "alpha male" of the OSS species marking out and guarding personal territory. Bezroukov (1999b) presents an example with an unhappy ending for one OSS developer:

> What "normally" happens to an open source development project when people writing code for it don't get along? How do open source authors deal with conflicts with other open source authors? Let me relate the story about my first experience maintaining open source software, as I think it's a pretty good illustration of this. I used to work on a program (for the sake of this discussion, let's call it P, for Program) that I volunteered to take over development work on around two years ago, after the original author produced version 1.0, and had no more time to work on P.

At the time I took over maintenance and development for the package, I had lots of time free at the business where I worked. My boss was understanding enough to allow me to devote a few hours a week of paid time to P, which I believe doesn't happen often for open source authors.

As time passed, our business grew, and I had less and less time to work on P. I managed to release an alpha version with some improvements, but some people weren't pleased with the pace of development. One of them took it upon himself to start work on his own version of P. For brevity, I'll call him Mr. J, for Jerk.

Now, normally I'd cheer this, since it's what open source is all about. However, it seemed what Mr. J really wanted was acclaim. I had released version 2.0 beta of P, based on the 1.0 version from the original author. Mr. J released a version he called P 1.2, also based on the original 1.0 code, with his own modifications. This generated a lot of confusion, at least in my opinion, since he had the same name for his package as mine, and similar version numbers. So, I asked him to please change the name of the package to something else to clear things up.

His response was to publicly declare that he should be named the official maintainer of P, since I was taking too long. I should note that at this point I would have happily turned over development to him, if I'd thought he could do the job well. I didn't think he could (putting it mildly). I'm going to skip over the discussion we had on the subject on the P mailing list (on my mail server) since it includes a lot of childishness on the part of Mr. J. Suffice it to say that things ended up with Mr. J calling me a few names, and vowing to take over P as part of a larger project he was working on.

Mr. J proceeded to take a copy of the names on my mailing list, and create his own list. He declared his version to be the official version of P, and ceased to take part in the original list I had set up. After all the argument on the original list, I was glad he was gone.

That is, until someone posted a question about my version of P to his list (which he had subscribed me to as well). He took the opportunity to publicly call me a few more names, and make some comments about my lack of progress. I had enough at this point, and mailed him telling him that I didn't want him to mention my name at all, ever again. I was hoping he'd start completely ignoring me, leaving me free to work on P quietly, without his interruptions.

Boy, was I wrong. Mr. J proceeded to mail me back and tell me that he would do whatever he pleased (again, putting it mildly). He also added a text description offering to let me perform an obscene act on him to his .sig file, which he used publicly on mailing lists and whatnot.

Completely appalled at this point, I e-mailed his providers for web space and connectivity, threatening them and him with lawsuits if he didn't remove my name from his postings. This got another nasty response from Mr. J, but eventually did get him to remove my name from his .sig file.

This brings me to present time. I now have such bad feelings associated with the whole affair that I don't like to think about P, much less work on it. I've stopped working publicly on it, in fact, and I only do development on in-house versions that will never see the light of day.

It is also questionable whether *all* OSS contributions are, in fact, valued equally. In the case of BSD, McKusick (1999) admits rather colorfully that 90 percent of contributions were thrown away, while "the rest were peed upon to make them smell like Berkeley." In a recent study of the Apache project, Mockus *et al.* (2000) found that almost 85 percent of modification requests by users were totally ignored. The same scenario is also borne out in the Orbiten Free Software Survey where it transpires that the top 10 developers (fewer than 0.1 percent of the total number of developers) contribute almost 20 percent of the code base (Ghosh and Prakash, 2000). Alan Cox, a main figure in Linux development, admits that most contributions are worthless, suggesting that they actually support the argument that one should need a license to get on the Internet, and that there are a lot of "dangerously half-clued people milling around," and that those of proven ability are well known within each product development community (Cox, 1998). Such evidence is not indicative of a collectivist atmosphere.

Likewise, there is evidence that the typical OSS developer is no longer an idealistic hacker working for free. As noted previously, an increasingly large group of developers are paid for their OSS work, with Jorgensen's (2001) survey of the FreeBSD project developers finding that 41 percent of developers were being paid.

The undoubted attraction of OSS to poorer institutions in the developing countries is paralleled by the extreme interest of fabulously wealthy institutions in the first world. As previously noted, OSS is of enormous interest to an organization like NASA, the US space agency, who desire complete transparency in the software they use, and believe that by having complete access to the source code, they can test it exhaustively themselves. Likewise the National Security Agency (NSA) has developed their own version of the Linux kernel. These are both examples of organizations that have sufficient resources to purchase any software they wish, and are quite far removed from any ideology of collectivism.

The rhetoric of the most prominent OSS spokesman, Eric Raymond, points to a related issue. Raymond (2001RotH) has admitted to being deliberately controversial – a media manipulation ploy – in his discussion of gun ownership. Statements like "Linux is about getting freedom, personal firearms are about keeping it"[4] are attention getting, but they are also significant. Rhetoric like this points to the libertarian (personal freedoms) rather than liberal (humanistic responsibility) philosophy that underpins the OSS agenda.

This confusion between libertarian and liberal has been perpetrated by many observers of the Open Source movement, who seem to associate it with a liberal ideology, albeit from geeks and nerds – a kind of "technical flower-power" caste, to use Torvalds' terminology (Torvalds and Diamond, 2001). However, much of open source is built on a libertarian pragmatism that quite comfortably accepts and, indeed, welcomes commercial exploitation of OSS products. However, it remains to be seen as to whether the great disparity of rewards, and the vast sums of money being made by some OSS pioneers, will erode the social fabric which holds the OSS process together.

---

[4] Article in *Atlanta Journal-Constitution*, August 21, 2000.

OSS vs. OSI vs. FSF

As we noted in Chapter 7, nowhere is the community tension more tangible than in the contestation between Free Software and Open Source ideologists. The delicate equilibrium of the pioneers of the OSS movement being able to cooperate and provide a unified front appears to have faltered lately. As mentioned before, Bruce Perens, one of the originators of the Open Source term and a significant contributor to establishing the movement through integrating it with the already viable *Debian Social Contract*, has resigned from the Open Source Initiative, amidst rumors of negative opinions about other OSS pioneers.[5] Also, Raymond has been forced to respond over and over again to criticisms that he has usurped too much of the OSS mantle.[6] Thus, it appears that individual egos (or at least the public perception of individual egos) cannot be as easily set aside in the interest of the movement as a whole as originally expected.

While the debate within the OSS community itself has been somewhat acrimonious at times, so also has there been considerable tension between the OSS and FSF communities. Richard Stallman's status has been eroded a little of late, although as previously noted, much of the software in the average Linux distribution is GNU. As noted in Chapter 7, Stallman continues to argue against the OSS label, suggesting that it ultimately raises more problems than it resolves.

---

[5] Slashdot (18/02/199) published an account of the acrimonious split, in which Perens is supposed to have labeled publisher and prominent OSS patron, Tim O'Reilly, as "one of the leading parisites (sic) of the free software community" (http://slashdot.org/articles/99/02/18/0927202.shtml). Another account of the more lurid details of the controversy (including Perens' fear for his safety due to Raymond's well-known expertise with a pistol) is provided in *Wired* at http://www.wired.com/news/technology/linux/story/19049.html

[6] http://www.tuxedo.org/~esr/writings/take-my-job-please.html

Is OSS a paradigm shift in software engineering?

The proponents of OSS point to the fact that very high quality software is being produced in a rapid time-scale and at little cost. These three aspects directly address the three main components of the so-called software crisis mentioned earlier. Thus, it would appear that OSS could be the "silver bullet" that can solve these problems. Further support comes from the arguments also put forward by the extreme proponents of OSS – that feedback is very prompt, the testing pool is global, peer review is truly independent, the contributors are in the top 5 percent of developers worldwide in terms of ability, and are self-selected and highly motivated. Given these factors, the argument that OSS truly is the "silver bullet" becomes even more cogent. However, the truly amazing aspect of OSS is that this "silver bullet" arises from a process that at first glance appears to be completely alien to the fundamental tenets and conventional wisdom of software engineering. For example, in the OSS process, there appears to be no real formal design process, no risk assessment nor measurable goals, no direct monetary incentives for developers or organizations, informal coordination and control, much duplication in parallel effort. All of these are anathema to conventional software engineering.

Also, as previously discussed, OSS appears to reverse Brook's Law (i.e., that adding manpower to a late software project makes it later), and the OSS community has proposed their own law, Linus's Law (i.e., given enough eyeballs, all bugs are shallow). Given these apparently contradictory axioms, one is reminded of Niels Bohr's contention that the opposite of a great truth is also true.

While the expected problems do not seem to manifest themselves in OSS, 30 years of software engineering research cannot be easily discounted. Thus, an examination of the details of the OSS development process serves to question the extent to which software engineering principles are actually being fundamentally overturned. Firstly, the main contributors of the OSS community are acknowledged to be superb coders, even if there is no direct evidence that they are actually among the top 5 percent of programmers in terms of their skills as some have claimed. Also, as they are self-selected, they are highly motivated to contribute. The remarkable potential of gifted individuals has long been recognized in the software engineering tradition. Brooks (1987) suggests that good programmers may be a hundred times more productive than mediocre ones. The Chief Programmer Team more than 20 years ago also bore witness to the potential of great programmers (Baker, 1972; Mills, 1971). Also, in more recent times, the capability maturity model (CMM) recognizes that fabulous success in software development has often been achieved due to the "heroics of talented individuals" (Paulk *et al.*, 1993). Thus, given the widely recognized talent of the OSS leaders, the success of OSS products may not be such a complete surprise.

The advancement of knowledge in software engineering has certainly been incorporated into OSS software. Linux, for example, benefited a great deal from the evolution of Unix in that defects were eliminated and requirements fleshed out a great deal (McConnell, 1999). Indeed, when one takes into account the massive resources which have been invested in Unix development, which Linux has been able to take full advantage of, then the comparison with the level of resources committed to proprietary software development by companies such as Microsoft is not as starkly different as might initially appear to be the case.

Furthermore, some of the fundamental concepts of software engineering in relation to cohesion and coupling and the modularity of code are very much a feature of OSS. Linux, by being based on Unix, is very modular in its architecture. Indeed, the manner in which different individuals can take responsibility for different self-contained modules within Linux is acknowledged as being a major factor in its successful evolution. In Open Source projects in general, as they mature, the learning curve increases in terms of under-standing the evolution of design requirements and product functionality. Thus, if new contributors are to have any hope of joining the project, some mechanism to reduce the overall learning curve is important. A subdivision of the overall project into smaller modules serves to reduce the amount of learning as new contributors can restrict their focus to a smaller set of modules. However, the extreme focus on modularity, while necessary, also represents a potential Achilles' heel for OSS, an issue discussed later in this chapter.

Further evidence of the importance of modularity arises from the Sendmail utility, first developed by Eric Allman at Berkeley in the late 1970s, with the source made available to interested parties. However, as it began to evolve through the contributions of others, problems in integrating contributions began to arise. Allman resigned from his position and rewrote Sendmail completely to follow a more modular structure. This ensured that it could be a suitable candidate for the massive parallel development, characteristic of OSS, as developers could work largely independently on different aspects. Sendmail has evolved to its current position of dominance – estimated to route 80 percent of all Internet mail. These examples provide much evidence that Open Source Software does obey the fundamental tenets of software engineering in relation to modularity. Indeed, the problems with the Mozilla project have been identified as stemming from the fact that the code was weakly modularized (Bollinger *et al.*, 1999).

Configuration management, another important research area within software engineering, is a vitally important factor within OSS, and is typically catered for by the Concurrent Versions System (CVS), itself an Open Source product (Fogel, 1999). Also, the software engineering principles of independent peer review and testing are very highly evolved to an extremely advanced level within OSS.

In summary, then, the code in OSS products is often very structured and modular in the first place; contributions are carefully vetted and incorporated in a very disciplined fashion in accordance with good configuration management, independent peer review, and testing. Thus, on closer inspection, the bazaar model of OSS does not seem to depart as wildly from many of the sensible and proven fundamental software engineering principles as was first assumed. The argument then that OSS begins as a bazaar with a chaotic development process and evolves mysteriously into a coordinated process with an exceptionally high-quality end-product is perhaps too simplistic a characterization of what actually is taking place in practice. Certainly, a study by McKenzie and Rouncefield (2001) of the Cocoon OSS project[7] reveals many continuities between traditional software engineering and Open Source development practice. Nevertheless, it is a paradox that while Linus Torvalds can effectively manage "the largest collaborative project in the history of humanity," his management of a small software team on a conventional development project at Transmeta was, by his own admission, something of a disaster (Torvalds and Diamond, 2001). This reinforces the view, discussed later in the chapter, that the success of the OSS model will not transfer seamlessly to software development in general, nor indeed to the wider work arena. Much more research is needed to achieve a better understanding of the phenomenon.

OSS and black boxes – The Berkeley Conundrum

The inherent invisibility of software (Brooks, 1987) is exacerbated by its distribution in binary form (1s and 0s), which is the necessary format for efficient computer operation. The availability of the actual source code certainly appears capable of redressing this invisibility. We would beg two questions related to this issue – is the availability of code a new concept, and how much impact does it have for the typical end user?

The concept of available source code is not revolutionary, although the OSS implementation of the concept may be. For example, the source code of many COTS products is often made available to preferred customers and development partners under NDAs (non-disclosure agreements). Likewise, it is common practice for custom-built software sold in binary form to have the source code held in escrow, thus protecting the purchaser in the event of the software vendor not surviving. What is different, of course, is that OSS grants users the freedom to change and redistribute the code – something definitely not granted by NDAs and code escrow arrangements.

---

[7] http://xml.apache.org/cocoon

While we can argue that OSS does, in fact, offer users unprecedented accessibility to code, we must still question how much impact this has in daily practice. For the common user of a large software package – a typical Linux distribution, for example, which contains more than 10 million lines of code – is the source code any more accessible than the binary executable? It has been argued that the most users (perhaps not always given the choice[8]) merely use OSS products in their binary executable form and ignore the source code (cf. Hissam and Weinstock, 2001). While users of OSS products certainly benefit indirectly from software enhancements made by others, not all – or indeed most – users benefit directly from the availability of code. We have coined the term, The Berkeley Conundrum, to represent this scenario, posing the question *if users do not actually download and modify the software source code, does it matter that it's open?* Further investigation is needed to determine to what extent users take advantage of (and perceive the value of) source code availability. Such research may help us determine whether OSS represents a paradigm shift in the nature of software distribution and consumption, as well as in the nature of software development.

> Berkeley, the eminent Irish philosopher, is associated with philosophical conundrums of the type: *if a tree falls in the forest, and there is no one to hear it, does it make a sound?* The Californian university is named after Berkeley, the philosopher, and it seems appropriate that this conundrum of Open Source should be termed The Berkeley Conundrum, given the prominent role of that institution in the OSS and free software movements. As an interesting footnote to a footnote, and with a view to promoting the discussion of gender issues in IS, Berkeley's classic conundrum has recently been recast as follows: *if a man speaks, and there is no woman present to hear, is he still wrong?*

One size fits all – is **OSS** the future of software?

One of the most critical questions regarding the future of OSS is whether or not it can be ported to the conventional software space.

---

[8] Downloading the full version of Linux over a standard telephone connection can take up to 36 hours, which is prohibitive for many would-be users.

Vixie (1999), for example, equates OSS development quite negatively as programming without rigor:

> Open Source developers often succeed for years before the difference between programming and software engineering finally catches up to them, simply because Open Source projects take longer to suffer from the lack of engineering rigor.

This sentiment is in keeping with that expressed by Ken Thompson which was presented at the beginning of this chapter, and also perhaps reinforces the findings of Stamelos *et al.* (2001) in relation to OSS software quality. However, much evidence has been presented in this book which would counter these negative opinions.

Some proponents of OSS have suggested that the incremental evolution that characterizes the development of OSS is actually quite similar to the development model of a proprietary software company such as Microsoft. For example, the core development team at Microsoft for Windows 2000 is estimated to have been in excess of 400 developers and 250 testers, and the beta release was then tested by over 100,000 users. This model is quite similar in some respects to the OSS development model. Also, the compelling evidence of successful examples of OSS could be used to argue that the approach needs to be more widely used. The argument often advanced is that software has zero reproduction costs but high service and maintenance costs, and the traditional model which is based on a high purchase fee and low maintenance fee is unsuited to the realities of the software business.

However, it is unrealistic to expect all software vendors to surrender the "crown jewels" in the intellectual property that resides in the software source code. Many in the OSS community accept that, and such a strategy is evident in the moves by some players in OSS to create a variation on the standard licenses to achieve this. Also, it appears that companies such as Apple with their Darwin MacOSX server, Netscape with Mozilla, and even Sendmail Pro, the commercial equivalent of Sendmail, are using OSS as a means of achieving some R&D, and then taking any useful updates provided by the OSS community back into their proprietary offerings.

If we consider the provenance of most OSS products, it boils down to Raymond's (2001CatB) memorable phrase "developers with a personal itch to scratch," a notion supported by many of the examples in this book. An examination of the products that have emerged reveals that the successful examples are typically general-purpose, horizontal infrastructure software. This is no accident. Given the finding by Jorgensen (2001), namely, that it is very rare to receive any feedback on design issues in OSS development, it would appear that OSS software is best suited to horizontal domains where design is almost a given, in that there is widespread agreement on design architecture, and the general shape of the software require-ments is fairly well known and not problematic. This is probably essential if contributions are to be drawn from developers with a wide variety of industry backgrounds and also from students and researchers in academe. On the other hand, in vertical domains where requirements and design issues are a function of specific domain knowledge that can only really be acquired over time – the case in many business environments, in fact – then there are not likely to be many OSS offerings.

One interesting exception to this, however, is the case of databases. These fall into the horizontal general-purpose software category. They may be complex software, but are no more so than an operating system, for example. However, there has not yet been significant market penetration of OSS databases (although mySQL is gaining in popularity and Red Hat's new offering is being aggressively marketed).

OSS certainly seems to be capable of generating revenue, profits, and investor support for some software organizations. However, the question remains as to whether it is truly sustainable from an economic point of view in the long term, particularly if it is expected to scale up to encompass the overall software industry. It is some-what paradoxical that in an initiative in which leadership is so central, that strategic direction, which normally comes from leaders, may be the Achilles' heel of OSS. That is, the organizing principle mentioned earlier, that of having a tail-light to follow, which appears to work well in coordinating individual developers towards a commonly shared development goal, may not be sufficient when strategic choices need to be made among competing sets of requirements for future development.

The discussion above would suggest that OSS is actually quite closely aligned to fundamental software engineering principles; thus, from that perspective, perhaps, there is less concern. Nevertheless, there would appear to be some serious software engineering concerns that need to be addressed. For example, as already mentioned, the OSS process for requirements analysis and design is not conducted in accordance with conventional software engineering principles. In relation to extending OSS products to a larger geographic area, issues such as internationalization and localization are not well covered in most existing OSS products (Wang and Whitehead, 2001). This could be potentially very serious as trying to accommodate such features is very difficult if they are not explicitly factored into the original design. The modification of Tcl to support the international Unicode standard required a drastic overhaul of the entire imple-mentation, for example. Also, the central importance of modularity in OSS product architecture has been repeatedly emphasized. Yet, in a recent comprehensive study of the Linux kernel, Schach *et al*. (2001) estimate that common coupling among modules has increased exponentially with each release, and they predict that this will make Linux very difficult to maintain without introducing regression faults in the future.

Also, while the motivations for contributing to OSS development discussed in Chapter 9 are quite powerful in themselves, if the OSS process is to challenge conventional software development, more mundane issues in relation to field support of OSS products must be provided. Lakhani and von Hippel (2000) investigate this issue in some detail in relation to the Apache Project, one of the most successful and widely used OSS products, but one where as the Apache group themselves explicitly state "there is no official support for Apache." Again, reinforcing the findings reported earlier in this chapter, Lakhani and von Hippel found that 25 percent of queries were ignored. More worryingly, there were no apparent differences in the types of queries that were answered and those that were ignored. Also, 50 percent of respondents to queries did so in less than 1 minute, while 96 percent of responses took less than 5 minutes. This suggests that those responding only considered queries for which the answers were ready to hand, and contrasts a great deal with the tale of the couch at the Microsoft user support center, which was apparently provided for those who had to provide telephone support for a particular function in a Microsoft product that was widely found to be problematic, and which required long and tedious explanation to users. Currently, the volume of queries on Apache is astonishingly small given its penetration and the volume of its user base. However, if the volume were to increase, the current mechanism would not be adequate. This situation is likely to be even more problematic for other OSS products. Thus, for these reasons, OSS has a large case to answer before one could be assured of its appropriateness as a model for software development in general.

There is also a delicate balance between reaping the advantages of having a multitude of developers contributing freely to an Open Source project and escaping the potential danger of serious bugs – hopefully inadvertent rather than malicious, but the latter cannot be completely ruled out – finding their way into the code. The InterNet News (INN) Usenet server offers an example of this, in that a serious bug was incorporated into the official release as part of a large patch that a user organization wanted to have incorporated. The resultant problems severely damaged INN's credibility, and it took three "good" releases subsequently to restore its reputation (Lawrence, 1998). Obviously, the traditional software development model is not immune to releasing buggy software, but the traditional process makes it perhaps less likely.

However, despite the somewhat mixed predictions for the future of OSS from a software engineering point of view, a very serious question mark remains in relation to social/human issues. This is an especial concern as the discussion above would reinforce the argument that OSS is much more a social innovation rather than a technical one. However, it may not be possible to maintain the delicate balance between the self-deprecation and modesty required to elicit cooperation in an OSS project, and the egoistic motivations that inevitably arise in a reputation-based culture. Add in the prospect of some "volunteers" making vast sums of money, and the balance becomes even more unstable. Furthermore, even if OSS developers manage to remain largely aloof from all this, the possibility of actual burn-out also is a factor. All of these issues appear to have happened or are imminent within OSS. Certainly, the biggest bottleneck in Linux development is now suggested to be Torvalds himself, who oversees all potential changes to the kernel, and receives a few hundred email messages a day in relation to this (Torvalds and Diamond, 2001).

Also, if the OSS movement is perceived as becoming part of the establishment, it could certainly lose some of its attraction to those renegades whose creative minds are probably its greatest asset.

Is OSS the future of work?

However, an even bigger question than whether OSS is merely a transitory software phenomenon ("the choice of a GNU generation"), is whether it represents the new mode of work for knowledge workers in the electronic age – a prospect that some researchers are beginning to hint at (Bollier, 1999; Dinkelacker and Garg, 2001; Gallivan, 2001; Himanen, 2001; Markus *et al.*, 2000; O'Reilly, 2000; Thompson, 2000). In a treatise outlining this future potential of OSS, Bollier (1999) states:

> ... a new and broader conversation must be started, one that considers the far-reaching implications of open code software for how we shall govern ourselves, improve education, foster innovation and economic growth, and protect the sovereign interests of citizens and consumers.

A project at the Berkman Center at the Harvard Law School[9] is investigating the transfer of the Open Source model to other areas,

---

[9] http://cyber.law.harvard.edu/mission/

including governance, education, economics, and law. The latter is especially interesting in that the parallels with software are readily apparent. As in software, there are an abundance of potential student contributors who can make significant intellectual contributions. Also, there is the dilemma between surrendering the secrecy aspects and the extra value that the volunteer contributors can bring in terms of elaborating the legal arguments. A supreme irony of the project is that one of its briefs is trying to find a remedy for Microsoft in their antitrust case.

Markus *et al.* (2000, p. 25) directly link the OSS model to the future of organizations:

> In short, there is a relatively high degree of correspondence between the open-source movement and popular depictions of the organization of the future and the virtual networked organization. Therefore, the open-source movement provides some suggestions about how management must change in the years a head. ... Although managers in industries *other* than software development may prefer more traditional styles of management, they should remember that the world is changing and workers are changing along with it. In a labor force of volunteers and virtual teams, the motivational and self-governing patterns of the open-source movement may well become essential to business success.

The transfer of the OSS hacker ethic beyond the confines of software and computing is also the goal of Himanen (2001) who conducts a very detailed analysis of the OSS hacker ethic, locating it in a historical context in relation to the Protestant work ethic and the pre-Protestant one, suggesting that it has more in common with the latter, and is more suited to the needs of the network society (Castells, 1996). Some of the characteristics of the hacker ethic are *passion* – the pursuit of a work agenda that is intrinsically motivating, and *freedom* – in the sense that work and leisure are not configured into a fixed routine but are dynamic and continuously optimized. These characteristics help to fuel the enormous creativity of OSS which has been discussed in the preceding chapters of this book.

Conclusion

We have raised the questions in this chapter, not to suggest that OSS is doomed – only that it is extremely complex. Future research into OSS must begin to ask increasingly difficult questions. The architectural characteristics and overall quality of OSS products need to be investigated and rigorously tested. The hybrid business models emerging, and their sustainability, need to be understood. The dialog between OSS and conventional software engineering needs to be progressed. And most importantly, we believe that the conflict and contestation within OSS communities needs to be addressed. OSS may be regarded as a software engineering paradigm shift, or a software business strategy revolution, but we believe that at its heart, it is a sociological phenomenon, which has potentially massive implications for the future of work and society.

Whether OSS represents the future of software or a transitory chapter in its history, this bigger question of the relevance of the OSS process to the future of work and society is an especially interesting one. Is the hacker/geek the carrier of the new order, and if so, is that a bad thing? Arriving at these questions has also been one of the primary purposes in writing this book.

References

Alexander, C., Ishikawa, S. and Silverstein, M. (1977) *A Pattern Language: Towns, Buildings, Construction*, Oxford: Oxford University Press.

Andersen, E. S. and Valente, M. (1999) "The two software cultures and the evolutionary economic simulation," http://www.business.auc.dk/~esa/evolution/esapapers/esa99/AndVal.pdf, Last Accessed June 21, 2001.

Aoki, A., Hayashi, K., Kishida, K., Nakakoji, K., Nishinaka, Y., Reeves, B., Takashima, A. and Yamamoto, Y. (2001) "A case study of the evolution of Jun: an object-oriented open-source 3D multimedia library," in *Proceedings of the 23rd International Conference on Software Engineering.* IEEE Computer Society, Los Alamitos, CA, pp. 524–33.

Apache Software Foundation (2001a) "Apache HTTP Server Version 2.0: Apache modules," http://httpd.apache.org/docs-2.0/mod/index.html, Last Accessed May 28, 2001.

Apache Software Foundation (2001b) "Apache project guidelines," http://dev.apache.org/guidelines.html, Last Accessed June 22, 2001.

Apache Software Foundation (2001c) "The Apache Software Foundation Board of Directors," http://www.apache.org/foundation/board/, Last Accessed June 9, 2001.

Apache Software Foundation (2001d) "Awards won by the Apache Web Server Software," http://www.apache.org/awards.html, Last Accessed May 8, 2001.

Apache Software Foundation (2001e) "Members of the Apache Software Foundation," http://www.apache.org/foundation/members.html, Last Accessed June 9, 2001.

Apache Software Foundation (2000) "Apache HTTP Server Project – Regular Contributors," http://httpd.apache.org/contributors/, Last Accessed June 13, 2001.

Ari, I. (2001) Quantitative analysis of open source software projects (personal communication).

Asklund, U. and Bendix, L. (2001) "Configuration management for open source software," in Feller, J., Fitzgerald, B. and van der Hoek, A. (eds), *Making Sense of the Bazaar: Proceedings of the 1st Workshop on Open Source Software Engineering*, available at http://opensource.ucc.ie/icse2001/.

Asundi, J. (2001) "Software engineering lessons from open source projects," in Feller, J., Fitzgerald, B. and van der Hoek, A. (eds) (2001) *Making Sense of the Bazaar*, *Proceedings of 1st Workshop on Open Source Software*, 23rd International Conference on Software Engineering, Toronto Canada, April 2001, available at http://opensource.ucc.ie/icse2001/papers.htm.

Avison, D., Golder, P. and Shah, H. (1992) "A toolkit for soft systems methodology", in Kendall, K., Lyytinen, K. and DeGross, H. (eds), *The Impact of Computer Supported Technologies on IS Development*, Elsevier Publishers, North Holland, 273–87.

Baker, F. (1972) "Chief Programmer Team management of production programming," *IBM Systems Journal*, **11**, 1, pp. 56–73.

Barahona, J.M.G., de las Heras Quiros, P., and Bollinger, T. (1999) "A brief history of free software and open source," *IEEE Software*, Jan/Feb.

Bergquist, M. and Ljungberg, J. (2001) "The power of gifts: organising social relationships in open source communities," *Information Systems Journal*, **11**, 4.

Bezroukov, N. (1999a) "A second look at the cathedral and the bazaar," *First Monday*, **4**, 12.

Bezroukov, N. (1999b) "Open source software as a special type of academic research (a critique of vulgar Raymondism)," *First Monday*, **4**, 10.

Bittman, M., Roos, R. and Kapfhammer, G.M. (2001) "Creating a free, dependable software engineering environment for building Java applications," in Feller, J., Fitzgerald, B. and van der Hoek, A. (eds), *Making Sense of the Bazaar: Proceedings of the 1st Workshop on Open Source Software Engineering*, available at http://opensource.ucc.ie/icse2001/papers.htm.

Bjorn-Andersen, N. (1988) "Are 'human factors' human?", *The Computer Journal*, **31**, 5, 386–90.

Blume, H. (1999) ExquisiteSource, *The Atlantic Online*, Aug. 12, at http://www.theatlantic.com/unbound/digicult/dc990812.htm, Last Accessed March 14, 2001.

Boehm, B. (1988) "A spiral model of software development and maintenance," *IEEE Computer*, **21**, 5, 61–72.

Boehm, B. (1981) *Software Engineering Economics*, Englewood Cliffs, NJ: Prentice Hall.

Boehm, B. (1976) "Software engineering," *IEEE Transactions on Computers*, **25**, 12, 1226–41.

Bokhari, S.H. and Rehman, R. (1999) "Linux and the developing world," *IEEE Software*, Jan/Feb.

Bollier, D. (1999) "The power of openness: why citizens, education, government and business should care about the coming revolution in open source code software", http://eon.law.harvard.edu/opencode/h20/.

Bollinger, T., Nelson, R., Self, K.M. and Turnbull, S.J. (1999) "Open-source methods: peering through the clutter," *IEEE Software*, Jul/Aug.

Borland, J. (2000) "Open-source MP3 project continues after parent's demise," *CNET News*, http://news.cnet.com/news/0-1005-200-4101023.html, Last Accessed June 8, 2001.

Box, G. (1979) "Robustness in the strategy of scientific model building," in Launer, R. and Wilkinson, G. (eds), *Robustness in Statistics*, New York: Academic Press.

Brooks, F. (1995) *The Mythical Man-Month*, Reading, MA: Addison-Wesley.

Brooks, F. (1987) "No silver bullet: essence and accidents of software engineering," *IEEE Computer Magazine*, April, 10–19.

Castells, M. (1996) *The Information Age: Economy, Society and Culture*. Vol. 1: *The Rise of the Network Society*, Malden, MA: Blackwell.

Checkland, P. (1994) "Notes on teaching and researching IS," *Systemist* (IS Special Edition Part II), **16,** 1, 6–8.

Checkland, P. (1981) *Systems Thinking, Systems Practice*, Chichester, Sussex: Wiley.

Checkland, P. and Holwell, S. (1998) *Information, Systems, and Information Systems: Making Sense of the Field*. Chichester, Sussex; New York: Wiley.

Checkland, P. and Scholes, J. (1990) *Soft Systems Methodology in Action*. Chichester, Sussex; New York: Wiley.

CMP (2001) "Open Source," *CMP's Techencyclopedia*, http://www.techweb.com/encyclopedia, Last Accessed May 24, 2001.

CNET Investor (2001) "Microsoft executive says Linux threatens innovation," http://www.cnetinvestor.com/investor/news/newsitem/ 0-9900-1028-4825719-0.html, Last Accessed February 27, 2001.

Computer User.com (2001) "Open Source software," *Computer User.com High Tech Dictionary*, http://www.computeruser.com/resources/ dictionary, Last Accessed May 24, 2001.

Cook, J. (2001) "Open source development: an Arthurian legend," in Feller, J., Fitzgerald, B. and van der Hoek A. (eds), *Making Sense of the Bazaar: Proceedings of the 1st Workshop on Open Source Software Engineering*, available at http://opensource.ucc.ie/icse2001/papers.htm.

Cosource.com (2001) "Cosource.com:Home:Browse Requests:Applications," http://www.cosource.com/cgi-bin/cos.pl/folder/info/1, Last Accessed May 24, 2001.

Cox, A. (1998) "Cathedrals, bazaars and the town council," http://slashdot.org/features/98/10/13/1423253.shtml, Last Accessed October 1, 2000.

Cubranic, D. (1999) Open-Source Software Development. ICSE 99 Workshop: *Software Engineering over the Internet*.

Dempsey, B.J., Weiss, D., Jones, P. and Greenberg, J. (1999) "A quantitative profile of a community of Open Source Linux developers," *Technical Report TR-1999-05, School of Information and Library Science, University of North Carolina at Chapel Hill*, http://ils.unc.edu/ils/ research/reports/TR-1999-05.pdf, Last Accessed April 24, 2001.

DiBona, C., Ockman, S. and Stone, M. (eds) (1999) *Open Sources: Voices from the Open Source Revolution*, Sebastapol, CA: O'Reilly.

Dinkelacker, J. and Garg, P.K. (2001) "Corporate source: applying open source concepts to a corporate environment," in Feller, J., Fitzgerald, B. and van der Hoek, A. (eds), *Making Sense of the Bazaar: Proceedings of the 1st Workshop on Open Source Software Engineering*, http://opensource.ucc.ie/icse2001

Dougherty, D. and Sims, D. (2000) "Will money spoil open source?", *O'Reilly Network*, http://www.oreillynet.com/pub/a/linux/2000/01/31/interview/ index.html, Last Accessed April 24, 2001.

Elgin, B. (1998) "Netscape to cut Mozilla's cord," *Sm@art Reseller*, *http://www.zdnet.com/zdnn/stories/news/0,4586,2176488,00.html*, Last Accessed July 4, 2001.

Feller, J. and Fitzgerald, B. (2000) "A framework analysis of the open source software development paradigm," *Proceedings of the 21st Annual International Conference on Information Systems*, pp. 58–69, http://afis.ucc.ie/jfeller/publications/ICIS2000.pdf, Last Accessed June 22, 2001.

Feller, J., Fitzgerald, B. and van der Hoek, A. (eds) (2001) *Making Sense of the Bazaar, Proceedings of 1st Workshop on Open Source Software, 23rd International Conference on Software Engineering*, Toronto, Canada, April 2001, available at http://opensource.ucc.ie/icse2001/.

Fielding, R.T. (1999) "Shared leadership in the Apache Project," *Communications of the ACM*, April, **42**, 4.

Fitzgerald, B. and Feller, J. (2001) "Open source software: investigating the software engineering, psychosocial and economic issues," *Information Systems Journal*, **11**, 4.

Fitzgerald, B. and Fitzgerald, G. (1999) "Categories and contents in IS development: making sense of the mess," in Ciberra, C. *et al.* (eds), *Proceedings of the 7th European Conference on Information Systems*, Copenhagen, Denmark, June, pp. 194–211.

Flaatten, P., McCubbrey, D., O'Riordan, P. and Burgess, K. (1989) *Foundations of Business Systems*, Chicago: Dryden Press.

Floyd, C., Melh, W., Resin, F., Schmidt, G. and Wolf, G. (1989) "Out of Scandinavia: alternative approaches to software design and system development," *Human Computer Interaction*, **4**, 253–350.

Fogel, K. (1999) *Open Source Development with CVS*, Scottsdale, AZ: Coriolis Group.

FOLDOC (2001a) "Open source," *FOLDOC: Free Online Dictionary of Computing*, http://foldoc.doc.ic.ac.uk/foldoc/index.html, Last Accessed May 24, 2001.

FOLDOC (2001b) "Open Source license," *FOLDOC: Free Online Dictionary of Computing*, http://foldoc.doc.ic.ac.uk/foldoc/index.html, Last Accessed May 24, 2001.

FreeBSD (2001) "The FreeBSD Committers' Big List of Rules," http://www.freebsd.org/tutorials/committers-guide/index.html.

Free Software Foundation (1996) "The Free Software Definition," http://www.fsf.org/philosophy/free-sw.html, Last Accessed June 1, 2001.

Freshmeat (2001a) "Browse Project Tree," http://freshmeat.net/browse/18/, Last Accessed May 24, 2001.

Freshmeat (2001b) "Browse Project Tree," http://freshmeat.net/browse/160/, Last Accessed May 24, 2001.

Friedman, A. (1989) *Computer Systems Development: History, Organisation and Implementation*, Chichester: Wiley and Sons.

Gacek, C., Lawrie, T. and Arief, B. (2001) The many meanings of open source, Department of Computing Science, University of Newcastle-upon-Tyne, Technical Report CS-TR-737, August.

Gallivan, M. (2001) "Striking a balance between trust and control in a virtual organization: a content analysis of open source software case studies," *Information Systems Journal*, **11**, 4.

Gamma, E., Helm, R., Johnson, R. and Vlissides, J. (1994) *Design Patterns*, Reading, MA: Addison Wesley Longman.

Ghosh, R. and Prakash, V.V. (2000) "The Orbiten Free Software Survey," *First Monday*, **5**, 7.

Glass, R.L. (2000) "The sociology of Open Source: of cults and cultures," *IEEE Software*, **17**, 3, 104–5.

Glass, R.L. (1999) "Of Open Source, Linux, … and Hype," *IEEE Software*, Jan/Feb.

Glass, R.L. (1998) "Is there really a software crisis?," *IEEE Software*, **15**, 1, 104–5.

Godfrey, M.W. and Lee, E.H.S. (2000) "Secrets from the monster: extracting Mozilla's software architecture," in *Proceedings of the Second International Symposium on Constructing Software Engineering Tools (CoSET'00)*, http://plg.uwaterloo.ca/~migod/papers/coset00.pdf, Last Accessed June 22, 2001.

Godfrey, M.W. and Tu, Q. (2000) "Evolution in Open Source software: A case study." Presented at *The 2000 International Conference on Software Maintenance*, http://plg2.math.uwaterloo.ca/~migod/papers/icsm00.pdf, Last Accessed June 22, 2001.

Goth, G. (2001) "The open market woos open source," *IEEE Software*, March/April, 104–7.

Hagel, J. and Armstrong, A.G. (1997) *Net Gain*, Boston, MA: HBS Press.

Halloween Documents (1998) "The Halloween Documents," http://www.opensource.org/halloween/, Last Accessed May 1, 2000.

Hamerly, J., Paquin, T. and Walton, S. (1999) "Freeing the source: the story of Mozilla," in DiBona, C., Ockman, S. and Stone, M. (eds) *Open Sources: Voices from the Open Source Revolution*, Sebastapol, CA: O'Reilly.

Hars, A. and Ou, S. (2001) "Working for free? – motivations of participating in Open Source projects," *Proceedings of 34th Hawaii International Conference on System Sciences,* Hawaii, January.

Hecker, F. (1999) "Setting up shop: the business of open-source software," *IEEE Software*, Jan/Feb.

Hermann, S., Hertel, G. and Niedner, S. (2000) "Linux study: first results," *Linux Study Home Page*, http://www.psychologie.uni-kiel.de/linux-study/writeup.html, Last Accessed April 24, 2001.

Himanen, P. (2001) *The Hacker Ethic*, Random House, New York.

Hissam, S.A. and Weinstock, C.B. (2001) "Open source software: the other commercial software," in Feller, J., Fitzgerald, B. and van der Hoek, A. (eds), *Making Sense of the Bazaar: Proceedings of the 1st Workshop on Open Source Software Engineering,* http://opensource.uc.ie/icse2001

Irwin, R. (1998) "What is FUD?", http://www.geocities.com/SiliconValley/Hills/9267/fuddef.html, Last Accessed May 1, 2000.

Jorgensen, N. (2001) "Putting it all in the trunk: incremental software development in the FreeBSD Open Source Project," *Information Systems Journal*, **11**, 4.

Kanellos, M. and Shankland, S. (1999) "Red Hat stock surge creates billionaires," *CNET News,* http://news.cnet.com/news/0-1003-200-113645.html, Last Accessed April 24, 2001.

Kawamoto, D. and Shankland, S. (1999) "VA Linux storms Wall Street with 698 percent gain," *CNET News*, http://news.cnet.com/news/0-1003-200-1489252.html, Last Accessed April 24, 2001.

Kay, M. (2001) "Soapbox: Reflections on open-source development," *IBM developerWorks*, http://www-106.ibm.com/developerworks/library/x-soapbx4.html, Last Accessed August 8, 2001.

Koch, S. and Schneider, G. (2001) "Effort, cooperation and coordination in an Open Source software project: GNOME", *Information Systems Journal*, **11**, 4.

Kuwabara, K. (2000) "Linux: a bazaar at the edge of chaos," *First Monday*, **5**, 3, http://firstmonday.org/issues/issue5_3/kuwabara/index.html, Last Accessed June 22, 2001.

Lakhani, K. and von Hippel, E. (2000) "How open source software works: free user to user assistance," Working Paper 41:7, MIT Sloan School of Management, Boston, MA.

Lawrence, D. (1998) "InternetNews server: inside an open-source project," *IEEE Internet Computing*, September–October, 49–52.

Lecht, C. (1977) *The Wars of Change*, New York: McGraw-Hill.

Leibovitch, E. (1999) "The business case for Linux," *IEEE Software*, Jan/Feb.

Leonard, A. (2000) *Salon Free Software Project*, http://www.salon.com/tech/fsp/, Last Accessed June 23, 2001.

Leonard, A. (1998) "Let my software go!", *Salon.com*, http://www.salon.com/21st/feature/1998/04/cov_14feature.html, Last Accessed June 21, 2001.

Lerner, J. and Tirole, J. (2000) "The simple economics of Open Source," Harvard Business School Working Paper #00-059.

Lewis, T. (1999) "The open source acid test," *IEEE Computer*, Feb.

Ljungberg, J. (2000) "Open Source movements as a model of organising," *European Journal of Information Systems*, **9**, 4.

Lyytinen, K., Rose, G. and Welke, R. (1998) "The brave new world of development in the internetwork computing architecture: or how distributed computing platforms will change systems development," *Information Systems Journal*, **8**, 3, 241–53.

MacEachern, D. (2001) "The Apache/Perl Module List," http://perl.apache.org/src/apache-modlist.html, Last Accessed May 24, 2001.

MacLachlan, M. (1999) "Panellists describe Open Source dictatorships," *TechWeb News*, http://www.techweb.com/wire/story/ TWB19990812S0003, Last Accessed May 30, 2001.

Markus, L., Manville, B. and Agres, C. (2000) "What makes a virtual organization work?", *Sloan Management Review*, **42**, 1, 13–26.

Maslow, A. (1970) *Motivation and Personality*, New York: Harper.

Masum, H. (2001) "Reputation layers for open-source development," in Feller, J., Fitzgerald, B. and van der Hoek, A. (eds), *Making Sense of the Bazaar: Proceedings of the 1st Workshop on Open Source Software Engineering*, http://opensource.ucc.ie/icse2001

Mauss, M. (1950) *The Gift: The Form and Reason for Exchange in Archaic Societies*, London: Routledge.

McConnell, S. (1999) "Open source methodology: ready for prime time?", *IEEE Software*, Jul/Aug.

McKenzie, A. and Rouncefield, M. (2001) "How 'hacking' hides a project: from software engineering to open source and back again" (personal communication).

McKusick, M. (1999) "Twenty years of Berkeley UNIX: from ATandT-owned to freely redistributable," in *Open Sources: Voices from the Open Source Revolution*, Sebastapol, CA: O'Reilly and Associates.

Mercurio, V., Meyers, B., Nisbet, A. and Radin, G. (1990) "AD/Cycle strategy and architecture", *IBM Systems Journal*, **29**, 2, 170–88.

Metcalfe, B. (1999) From the ether, June 21, http://www.infoworld.com/cgi-bin/displayNew.pl?/metcalfe/990621bm.htm.

Microsoft (2001) "Microsoft affirms commitment to shared source," http://www.microsoft.com/BUSINESS/licensing/sharedsource/commitment.asp, Last Accessed May 24, 2001.

Mills, H. (1971) "Chief programmer teams: principles and procedures," IBM Federal Systems Division, Gaithersburg, US.

Mockus, A., Fielding, R. and Herbsleb, J. (2000) "A case study of Open Source software development: the Apache server," in *Proceedings of 22nd International Conference on Software Engineering*, IEEE Computer Society, Los Alamitos, CA, pp. 263–72.

Montgomery, S. (1991) *AD/Cycle: IBM's Framework for Application Development and Case*, New York: Van Nostrand Reinhold.

Moody, G. (1997) "The Greatest OS That (N)ever Was," *Wired*, 5.08.

Moon, J.Y. and Sproull, L. (2000) "Essence of distributed work: the case of the Linux kernel," *First Monday*, **5**, 11, http://firstmonday.org/issues/issue5_11/ moon/index.html, Last Accessed April 20, 2001.

Mozilla Organization (2001) "Getting involved with mozilla.org," http://mozilla.org/get-involved.html, Last Accessed June 20, 2001.

Nakakoji, K. and Yamamoto, Y. (2001) "Taxonomy of open source software development," in Feller, J., Fitzgerald, B. and van der Hoek, A. (eds), *Making Sense of the Bazaar: Proceedings of the 1st Workshop on Open Source Software Engineering*, http://opensource.ucc.ie/icse2001

Netcraft (2001a) "The Netcraft Web Server Survey," http://www.netcraft.com/survey/, Last Accessed April 24, 2001.

Netcraft (2001b) "Sites with longest running systems by average uptime in the last 90 days," http://uptime.netcraft.com/up/today/top.avg.html, Generated on May 30, 2001.

Neumann, P.G. (2000a) "The potentials of open-box source code in developing robust systems," *NATO Conference*, April 2000.

Neumann, P.G. (2000b) "Robust nonproprietary software," *IEEE Symposium on Security and Privacy*, May.

Neumann, P.G. (1998) "Robust open-source software," *Communications of the ACM*, February, **41**, 2.

Niedner, S. (2000) "Linux Study: raw data," *Linux Study Home Page*, http://www.psychologie.uni-kiel.de/linux-study/questionnaire.dat, Last Accessed April 24, 2001.

Niedner, S., Hertel, G. and Hermann, S. (2000) "Motivation in Open Source Projects," *Presentation at the Nijmegen Business School*, http://www.psychologie.uni-kiel.de/~niedner/nijmegen.ppt, Last Accessed April 24, 2001.

Norin, A. L. and Stöckel, F. (1998) *Open Source Development Methodology*, University of Luleå, Sweden, May.

Open Source Initiative (2001a) "The Approved Licenses," http://opensource.org/licenses/index.html, Last Accessed May 8, 2001.

Open Source Initiative (2001b) "History of the OSI," http://www.Open Source.org/docs/history.html, Last Accessed April 24, 2001.

Open Source Initiative (2001c) "The Open Source Definition (Version 1.8)," http://www.opensource.org/docs/definition.html, Last Accessed April 24, 2001.

Open Source Initiative (2001d) "OSI Certification Mark and Program," http://www.opensource.org/docs/certification_mark.html, Last Accessed May 8, 2001.

Open Source Initiative (2001e) "The Open Source Initiative: Frequently

Asked Questions", http://www.opensource.org/advocacy/faq.html, Last Accessed May 8, 2001.

O'Reilly, T. (2000) "Open source: the model for collaboration in the age of the Internet," Wide Open News, http://www.wideopen.com/reprint/740.html, Last Accessed May 1, 2000.

O'Reilly.com (1998) "Freeware leaders meet in first-ever summit," http://press.oreilly.com/freeware.html, Last Accessed May 8, 2001.

Paulk, M., Curtis, B., Chrissis, M. and Weber, C. (1993) "Capability Maturity Model for Software, version 1.1," *IEEE Software*, **10**, 4, 18–27.

Perens, B. (1999) "The Open Source Definition," in DiBona, C., Ockman, S. and Stone, M. (eds) *Open Sources: Voices from the Open Source Revolution*, Sebastapol, CA: O'Reilly, pp. 171–88.

Pfaff, B. and David, K. (1998) "Society and Open Source: why Open Source software is better for society than closed source software," http://www.msu.edu/user/pfaffben/writings/anp/oss-is-better.html.

PITAC (2000) *Open Source Software for High End Computing*, http://www.ccic.gov/pubs/pitac/pres-oss-11sep00.pdf, Last Accessed August 2, 2001.

Raymond, E.S. (2001) *The Cathedral and the Bazaar: Musings on Linux and Open Source by an Accidental Revolutionary*, Sebastapol, CA: O'Reilly.

Raymond, E.S. (ed.)(2001JFa) Open Source, *Jargon File VERSION 4.3.0*, http://www.tuxedo.org/~esr/jargon, Last Accessed May 8, 2001.

Raymond, E.S. (ed.)(2001JFb) suit, *Jargon File VERSION 4.3.0*, http://www.tuxedo.org/~esr/jargon, Last Accessed May 8, 2001.

Raymond, E.S. (2001BHH) "A Brief History of Hackerdom," in Raymond, E.S. (2001), *The Cathedral and the Bazaar: Musings on Linux and Open Source by an Accidental Revolutionary*, Sebastapol, CA: O'Reilly, pp. 1–18.

Raymond, E.S. (2001CatB) "The Cathedral and the Bazaar," in Raymond, E.S. (2001), *The Cathedral and the Bazaar: Musings on Linux and Open Source by an Accidental Revolutionary*, Sebastapol, CA: O'Reilly, pp. 19–64.

Raymond, E.S. (2001HtN) "Homesteading the Noosphere," in Raymond, E.S. (2001), *The Cathedral and the Bazaar: Musings on Linux and*

Open Source by an Accidental Revolutionary, Sebastapol, CA: O'Reilly, pp. 65–112.

Raymond, E.S. (2001MC) "The Magic Cauldron," in Raymond, E.S. (2001), *The Cathedral and the Bazaar: Musings on Linux and Open Source by an Accidental Revolutionary*, Sebastapol, CA: O'Reilly, pp. 113–66.

Raymond, E.S. (2001RotH) "Revenge of the Hackers," in Raymond, E.S. (2001), *The Cathedral and the Bazaar: Musings on the Linux and Open Source by an Accidental Revolutionary*, Sebastapol, CA: O'Reilly, pp. 167–92.

Raymond, E.S. (1999) "Shut up and show them the code," http://www.tuxedo.org/~esr/writings/shut-up-and-show-them.html, Last Accessed June 1, 2001.

Raymond, E.S. (1997) "The Cathedral and the Bazaar (Revision 1.16)," http://www.tuxedo.org/˜esr/writings/

Red Hat (2001a) "Red Hat achieves positive cash flows from operations and shows a profit for the first time in first quarter," http://redhat.com/about/presscenter/2001/press_Q12002.html, Last Accessed June 22, 2001.

Red Hat (2001b) *Red Hat Linux 6.0: The Official Red Hat Linux Installation Guide*, http://www.redhat.com/support/manuals/RHL-6.0-Manual/install-guide/manual, Last Accessed May 24, 2001.

Rheingold, H. (1994) *The Virtual Community*, Great Britain: Minerva.

Rosen, L.E. (2001) "RE: trademarked logos and GPL," http://www.mail-archive.com/license-discuss@opensource.org/msg02746.html, Last Accessed August 8, 2001.

Rosenberg, D.K. (2000) *Open Source: The Unauthorized White Papers*, Foster City, CA: IDG.

Russo, N., Fitzgerald, B. and DeGross, J. (eds) (2001) *Realigning Research and Practice in Information Systems Development: The Social and Organizational Perspective*, Boston: Kluwer Academic Press.

Sanders, J. (1998) "Linux, open source, and software's future," *IEEE Software*, Sept/Oct.

Scacchi, W. (2001) Understanding requirements for developing open source software systems, Institute for Software Research Working Paper Scacchi-2001-07, University of California, Irvine.

Schach, S., Jin, B. and Wright, D. (2001) Maintainability of the Linux kernel, Technical Report {ISE-TR-01-04}, Department of Information and Software Engineering, George Mason University.

Schmerken, I. (2000) "Open-source investing: is Wall Street's research game over?", *Wall Street and Technology*, **18**, 8, 66–8.

Schmidt, D.C. and Porter, A. (2001) "Leveraging open-source communities to improve the quality & performance of open-source software," in Feller, J., Fitzgerald, B. and van der Hoek, A. (eds), *Making Sense of the Bazaar: Proceedings of the 1st Workshop on Open Source Software Engineering*, htp://opensource.ucc.ie/icse2001

Sessions, R. (1999) "A lesson from Palm Pilot," *IEEE Software*, **16**, 1, 36–8.

Shankland, S. (2001) "Linux growth underscores threat to Microsoft," *CNET News*, http://news.cnet.com/news/0-1003-200-4979275.html, Last Accessed April 24, 2001.

Shankland, S. (1999) "Red Hat shares triple in IPO," *CNET News*, http://news.cnet.com/news/0-1003-200-345929.html, Last Accessed April 24, 2001.

Shaw, M. and Garlan, D. (1996) *Software Architecture: Perspectives on an Emerging Discipline*, Upper Saddle River, NJ: Prentice-Hall.

Smith, C.S. (2000) "China moves to cut power of Microsoft," *The New York Times*, July 8.

Smith, M. and Kollock, P. (eds) (1999) *Communities in Cyberspace*, London: Routledge.

Smyth, J. (2001) "Interview with Robert McDowell, Microsoft Vice President Worldwide Services," *The Irish Times*, June 1.

Sowa, J. and Zachman, J. (1992) "Extending and formalizing the framework for IS architecture," *IBM Systems Journal*, **31**, 3, 590–616.

Stallman, R.M. (2001a) "Categories of free and non-free software," http://www.gnu.org/philosophy/categories.html, Last Accessed May 24, 2001.

Stallman, R.M (2001b) "The problems of the Apple Licence," http://www.fsf.org/philosophy/apsl.html, Last Accessed May 24, 2001.

Stallman, R.M. (1999a) "The GNU operating system and the Free Software Movement," in DiBona, C., Ockman, S. and M. Stone (eds), *Open Sources*, Sebastapol, CA: O'Reilly, pp. 53–70.

Stallman, R.M. (1999b) "RMS responds," *Slashdot*, http://slashdot.org/articles/99/06/28/1311232.shtml, Last Accessed June 1, 2001.

Stallman, R.M. (1999c) "Why you shouldn't use the Library GPL for your next library," http://www.fsf.org/philosophy/why-not-lgpl.html, Last Accessed May 29, 2001.

Stallman, R.M. (1998) "Why 'Free Software' is better than 'Open Source'," http://www.fsf.org/philosophy/free-software-for-freedom.html, Last Accessed June 1, 2001.

Stallman, R. (1992) "Why software should be free," http://www.fsf.org/philosophy/shouldbefree.html, Last Accessed April 24, 2001.

Stallman, R. (1985) "The GNU Manifesto," http://www.fsf.org/gnu/manifesto.html, Last Accessed June 22, 2001.

Stamelos, I., Angelis, L. Oikonomou, A. and Bleris, G. (2002) Code Quality Analysis in Open-Source Software Development, *Information Systems Journal*, **12**, 1.

Tauber, J. (1999) "Open Source Software Engineering," *FoRK Archive*, http://www.xent.com/sept99/0405.html, Last Accessed April 24, 2001.

Taylor, T. and Standish, T. (1982) "Initial thoughts on rapid prototyping techniques," *ACM SIGSOFT Software Engineering Notes*, **7**, 5, 160–6.

Thompson, K. (1999) "Unix and beyond: an interview with Ken Thompson," *IEEE Computer*, May, http://computer.org/computer/thompson.htm.

Thompson, N. (2000) "Reboot! How Linux and open-source development could change the way we get things done," *The Washington Monthly*, http://www.washingtonmonthly.com/features/2000/0003.thompson.html, Last Accessed June 3, 2001.

Torvalds, L. (1998) "What motivates free developers?", Interview in *First Monday*, http://firstmonday.org/issues/issue3_3/torvalds/index.html, Last Accessed July 4, 2001.

Torvalds, L. and Diamond, D. (2001) *Just for Fun: The Story of an Accidental Revolutionary*, New York: HarperCollins.

Tran, J.B., Godfrey, M.W., Lee, E.H.S. and Holt, R.C. (2000) "Architecture repair of open source software," in *Proceedings of the 2000 International Workshop on Program Comprehension (IWPC'00)*. Presentation in Limerick, Ireland.

Travis, G. (2001) "Emacs a top-notch Java IDE? You bet!", http://www-106.ibm.com/developerworks/java/library/j-emacs/, Last Accessed June 23, 2001.

VA Linux (2001) "VA Linux outlines new strategic focus on software," http://www.valinux.com/about/news/releases/062701.html, Last Accessed August 8, 2001.

van der Hoek, A. (2000) "Configuration management and open source projects," ICSE 2000 Workshop: *Software Engineering over the Internet*. Presentation in Limerick, Ireland.

Vitalari, N. and Dickson, G. (1983) "Problem solving for effective systems analysis: an experimental exploration," *Communications of the ACM*, November, 948–56.

Vixie, P. (1999) "Software engineering," in DiBona *et al.* (1999).

Wall, L. (1999) "Diligence, patience and humility," in DiBona *et al.* (1999), pp. 127–48.

Wang, E. and Whitehead, E. (2001) International accessibility of open source software (personal communication).

Webopedia (2001) "Open Source", *Webopedia,* http://www.webopedia.com/TERM/o/open_source.html, Last Accessed May 8, 2001.

Weinberg, G. (1971) *The Psychology of Computer Programming*, New York: Rheinhold.

Whatis?com (2001) "Open source," *Whatis?com TechTarget*, http://whatis.techtarget.com/ Open Source, Last Accessed May 8, 2001.

Williams, S. (2000) Open season: learning the ways of Mozilla, Upside Today: The Tech Insider, http://www.upside.com, Last Accessed October 12, 2000.

Wilson, B. (1984) *Systems: Concepts, Methods and Applications*, Maidenhead: Wiley.

Wilson, G. (1999) "Is the Open Source community setting a bad example?", *IEEE Software*, **16**, 1, 23–5.

Wilson, J. (2001) "Editors' Choice Awards – Best in Java", *Java World*, http://www.javaworld.com/javaworld/javaone01/j1-01-awards.html, Last Accessed June 11, 2001.

Yee, D. (1999) "Development, ethical trading and free software," *First Monday*, Issue 4_12, http://firstmonday.org/issues/issue4_12/yee/index.html, Last Accessed July 4, 2001.

Young, R. (1999) "Giving it away: how Red Hat Software stumbled across a new economic model and helped improve an industry," in DiBona, C., Ockman, S. and Stone, M. (eds) *Open Sources: Voices for the Open Source Revolution*, Sebastapol, CA: O'Reilly.

Young, R. and Rohm, W.G. (1999) *Under the Radar*, Scottsdale, AZ: Coriolis Group.

Zachman, J. (1987) A framework for IS architecture, *IBM Systems Journal*, **26**, 3, 276–92.

Zope.org (2001a) "Zope Public License," http://www.zope.org/Resources/License, Last Accessed May 8, 2001.

Zope.org (2001b) "Zope Public License (ZPL) Version 1.0," http://www.zope.org/Resources/ZPL, Last Accessed May 8, 2001.

Index